ON CHRISTIAN DOCTRINE

The Library of Liberal Arts
OSKAR PIEST, FOUNDER

ON CHRISTIAN DOCTRINE

SAINT AUGUSTINE

Translated, with an introduction, by

D. W. ROBERTSON, JR.

The Library of Liberal Arts
published by

Bobbs-Merrill Educational Publishing
Indianapolis

Saint Augustine: 354-430

. . . .

The Bobbs-Merrill Company, Inc.
4300 West 62nd Street
Indianapolis, Indiana 46268

First Edition

Fourteenth Printing—1977

Library of Congress Catalog Card Number: 58–9956
ISBN 0–672–60262–8 (pbk)
ISBN 0–672–51031–6

TRANSLATOR'S PREFACE

This translation of St. Augustine's *De doctrina Christiana* is based on the Benedictine text. Quotations from the Bible appear in the Douay-Rheims version, but the footnotes contain references in brackets to indicate the location of corresponding verses in the King James Bible where that Bible contains the same material arranged according to a different system. These quotations have not been altered so as to conform exactly to St. Augustine's text except in those instances where such alterations were necessary for clarity. In the process of this work I have consulted, from time to time, the earlier English versions of Shaw and Gavigan, and I gratefully acknowledge that I derived considerable assistance in clearing up a number of difficult or ambiguous passages.

There are innumerable ways of approaching a work of such fundamental importance as this one. In the Introduction which follows I have emphasized the significance of *On Christian Doctrine* during the Middle Ages, when it exerted its greatest influence. However, the reader who is interested in the text for other reasons may easily disregard this material. Some of the books mentioned in the last paragraph of the Introduction contain extensive lists of references. As for the translation itself, anyone familiar with the problems involved in rendering a work of this kind into English will understand that the translator can only hope that if St. Augustine were able to read his work, he would not find occasion on every page to refer to Martial's epigram to Fidentius, in slightly altered form:

> The work you recite is mine, O translator,
> But when you recite it badly it begins to be yours.

I should like to express my indebtedness to the readers for "The Library of Liberal Arts" who made many useful suggestions for revisions in the first draft of this translation. In particular, I am grateful to Mr. Oskar Piest, whose unfailing good will made this book possible.

D. W. ROBERTSON, JR.

COMBE LONGA, OXFORDSHIRE
Feb. 15, 1958

CONTENTS

TRANSLATOR'S INTRODUCTION

On Christian Doctrine was begun *c.* 396 at about the time St. Augustine became bishop of Hippo. The work was carried only through paragraph 35 of Book III. But in 427, in the course of writing the *Retractions*, St. Augustine took it up again, adding the final sections of Book III and the whole of Book IV. At the same time, he indicated certain revisions in the earlier part of the work, but did not incorporate them in the text. Specifically, he pointed out that the attribution of the Book of Wisdom to Jesus son of Sirach (2. 8. 13) is probably false; that although the term "Old Testament" is used by the Church to designate the forty-four books he mentions, apostolic language restricts it to the Tables of the Law; and, finally, that he had misrepresented St. Ambrose with reference to the relationship between Plato and Jeremias (2. 28. 43). The book thus completed and revised is among the most important writings of the most influential of the Fathers of the Christian Church. Indeed, it has been said to provide "the fundamental plan of Christian culture."

Essentially, *On Christian Doctrine* is an introduction to the interpretation and explanation of the Bible. For St. Augustine interpretation was not something to be controlled exclusively by scientific techniques of philological and historical analysis; these were but adjuncts to a task whose purposes could be met only through a knowledge of the philosophical principles implied or stated by the authors of the New Testament. We do not always realize today the extent to which the theology of Christianity was at once a logical outgrowth of late classical thought and, at the same time, an astonishingly brilliant fulfillment of the best traditions of ancient philosophy as they extend from Pythagoras and Plato to Cicero and Varro. Paganism, as a great classical scholar has said, "groped and staggered in the pursuit of an ideal concerning which it could have only an obscure prescience. But when the message of the gospel reached its best thinkers, they believed that they had finally attained it in the flash of certainty which suddenly struck them." [1] St. Augustine was pre-eminent among those Christian writers in the West who set before themselves the task of elaborating the new philosophy, and *On Christian Doctrine* offers abundant evidence of an intellectual acumen which had a large share in creating the pattern of a culture which endured in the West throughout the thousand years we rather unjustly call "the Middle Ages." It formulates an approach to the Scriptures whose principles determined the character of education during that period; and the ideal of *sapientia et eloquentia,* "wisdom and eloquence," adapted from Cicero and here given a Christian fulfillment, was still an important part of Christian humanism in the Renaissance.

Underlying the specific techniques of both interpretation and exposition of Scripture the principle of first importance in St. Augustine's mind is charity.[2] The introduction and spread of this specifically Christian doctrine marks the decisive break between antiquity and the Middle Ages. But at the same time there is much in the philosophy, literature, and religion of antiquity which looks forward to it, almost as if in search of it. Whether we are considering the plays of Euripides, the Socratic dialogues, Cicero's treatise on friendship, the poetry of Virgil or Ovid, or the cults of Asclepius or Hercules, we can detect without too much difficulty a quest for a love which will lead neither to those aberrations so amusingly described in the *Ars amatoria* nor to the jealous strife of Trojan wars, but which will unify human society in a peaceful and reasonable order where love and compassion can exist without either malice or unmanly sentimentality. To Christian thinkers of late antiquity, charity was the gift of the Holy Spirit sent by Christ by means of which such an order could be established, if not in the temporal world, at least in the spiritual

1 Jérome Carcopino, *De Pythagore aux Apôtres* (Paris, 1956), p. 80.
2 For a definition, see 3. 10. 16. The subject is discussed very fully in St. Augustine's commentary on the Epistles of St. John.

world of the Church made up of those united in Christ. Here it was, for example, that Lactantius saw the return of the Golden Age. Hence it was not surprising that St. Augustine should seek this doctrine in the Old Testament, using for this purpose an allegorical method of interpretation, for the writings therein embodied were also inspired by the Holy Spirit. To discover it there as allegorical prophecy and foreshadowing after the manner of St. Paul [3] was simply to discover the fulfillment of the Law as Christ had promised it. And to demand it as an underlying principle of Christian writings, even of an Ovidian fable like that by St. Augustine's friend Licentius,[4] was simply to demand that they be Christian.

St. Augustine's exegetical principles have been characterized by modern writers as "fantastic" or "unscientific," and efforts have been made to explain them away as the result of his early rhetorical training or of the "decadence" of the period during which he wrote. However, St. Augustine's use of allegory adheres closely to the methods suggested in the Pauline epistles and in utterances like that in Matt. 22. 43-44. He found his initial inspiration, moreover, in the sermons of St. Ambrose, which gave to the Old Testament an unexpected philosophical integrity, rather than in pagan allegories. Again, scientific philology is obviously not a road to charity. For St. Augustine, empirical knowledge pursued for its own sake "puffeth up"; wisdom, on the other hand, seeks to discover through "the things that are made," not their accidental properties, but the "invisible things" of God.[5] If the allegorical method fails to produce a single "correct" interpretation for each passage but leads instead to the perception of a diversity of meanings, some of which may not have been intended by the author, this fact is regarded by St. Augustine not as a shortcoming but as a virtue, provided that all of these meanings are supported in other parts of the Scriptures. For although the Scriptures are the work of a variety of human

[3] See especially Gal. 4. 21-31.
[4] *De ordine* 1. 8. 24.
[5] Rom. 1. 20. See 1. 4. 4 and 2. 41. 62.

authors, they have a single divine inspiration and may hence be considered as a work of unified intention. When we discover a meaning consistent with the whole but not intended by the human author, that meaning may be thought of as intended by the Divine Author, "who undoubtedly foresaw that this meaning would occur to the reader or listener" (3. 27. 38). In short, St. Augustine's method is based on that faith, hope, and charity which he so masterfully describes in Book I, and on a wholehearted trust in Providence rather than in science. It may not be a method suited to our times, but it was a method eminently suited to his time and place. If we wish to understand him, we should make an effort to regard it with at least an historical sympathy.

On Christian Doctrine exerted an enormous influence throughout the Middle Ages. It formed the basis for the *De institutione divinarum et secularium litterarum* of Cassiodorus, and whole sections of it were incorporated in the *De clericorum institutione* of Rabanus Maurus. In the twelfth century it provided the inspiration for the *Didascalicon* of Hugh of St. Victor, and it contributed the organizing principles to the *Sententiae* of Peter Lombard. The spiritual interpretation of Scripture, whose methods it establishes, continued to flourish well into the seventeenth century, even though more literal approaches were developed in academic circles during the thirteenth century. Much of the *Glossa ordinaria,* which was a basic aid to scriptural study after the twelfth century, represents the work of St. Augustine himself or of expositors who were either influenced by him or employed similar methods. Among prominent later spiritual exegetes were St. Bonaventura, Grosseteste, Holcot, Bersuire, and Erasmus. *On Christian Doctrine* was endorsed by Wiclif, commended to the readers of the Wiclifite Bible, and translated by John Purvey. Erasmus refers to the obscurity of Scripture which St. Augustine "brilliantly explains in his work *On Christian Doctrine.*" [6] Perhaps no better evidence for the enthusiasm with which

---

[6] *Ecclesiastae* 3.

some writers defended the spiritual sense against encroaching literalism in the early Renaissance may be found than the statement by Erasmus in the *Enchiridion* to the effect that it is more profitable to read a single verse of a Psalm spiritually than to read the whole Psalter literally.

Historians of art and literature should find *On Christian Doctrine* especially helpful to an understanding of medieval culture. In recent years the study of iconology has become a very fruitful branch of art history, and many studies have appeared in the wake of the spectacular success achieved by Emile Mâle. The symbolic techniques of medieval art are essentially analogous with the symbolic techniques of scriptural interpretation, even in those instances where classical allegories are simply copied to have their significance transformed by Christian implications, as they are, for example, on certain early funerary monuments. The task of the iconologist is facilitated if he is able, not only to discover the significance of specific symbols, but also to understand the rationale which underlies their use. No better introduction to that rationale may be found than *On Christian Doctrine*. Needless to say, much of the symbolism that appears in art also appears in literary texts.

In so far as the preservation of classical art and literature is concerned, St. Augustine's statement that "every good and true Christian should understand that wherever he may find truth, it is his Lord's" (2. 18. 28) has frequently been cited as the watchword of Christian humanism. The argument involving "Egyptian gold" (2. 40. 60), in accordance with which Christians are urged to adapt whatever pagan ideas or institutions they may find suitable to their purposes, was repeated over and over by writers who either used classical literature and philosophy in their own work or saw fit to write commentaries on classical texts. As we might expect, these commentaries frequently reflect the same general techniques that St. Augustine applied to the Scriptures, with the reservation, not always strictly adhered to, that since such texts were not divinely inspired, they were susceptible only to verbal analysis and not to an analysis of the "things" underlying the words. But it is wrong to see in such writers as Theodulf of Orléans or his successor in the school of Orléans, Arnulf, or Albericus of London, or John of Salisbury, or Bersuire, or Boccaccio, or Ficino a "tension" between Christianity on the one hand and paganism on the other. St. Augustine's encouragement is clear enough, and his own copious use of Cicero and Virgil offers a sufficiently plain example. The transformation of Ciceronian rhetoric for Christian orators in Book IV of *On Christian Doctrine* sets a typical precedent for medieval humanistic activity. Meanwhile, it should not be forgotten that the allegorical interpretation of literature was a classical practice, begun perhaps as early as the sixth century B.C. by the Pythagoreans and continued in late antiquity by Neopythagoreans, Stoics, and Neoplatonists, all of whom were interested in the preservation of literature because of the philosophical values they found in it. It is not surprising that Christian writers should have used similar techniques and, indeed, sometimes reached conclusions very like those of their classical predecessors in their search for truth buried in the fables of the classical poets, as if digging it up, as St. Augustine would say, "from certain mines of Divine Providence, which is everywhere infused "

Finally, *On Christian Doctrine* illustrates and describes a literary aesthetic which has much to do with the general character of early Western art and literature. The relevant passage is that in 2. 6. 7-8 where the assertion that the obscurity of Scripture is both pleasant and useful is illustrated by an analysis of a passage from the Canticle. Several features of this illustration deserve comment.[7] St. Augustine says, "I contemplate the saints more pleasantly when I envisage them as the teeth of the Church," and again, "I recognize them most pleasantly as shorn sheep." It will be seen at once that the idea of saints as "teeth" or as "shorn sheep" does not belong to the same

[7] If we dismiss it on the grounds that it is merely a reflection of Jewish and pagan techniques (which it is not), we shall close our minds to an understanding of much of St. Augustine's exegesis as well as to that of many of his followers.

order of phenomena as the feeling conveyed by "my love is like a red, red rose." There is no spontaneous emotional appeal in St. Augustine's comparisons of the kind we expect in modern poetry. They do not, to use a phrase from Godwin, "awaken the imagination, astound the fancy, or hurry away the soul." Indeed, if we read what St. Augustine says about these figures with either modern romantic expectations or modern rationalistic expectations, it seems ridiculous. However, we should realize that romantic metaphor would have appeared laughable, or, perhaps, lamentable, to him and that he would have regarded the modern scientific conscience as a form of slavery. The appeal of the Augustinian comparison lies in an intellectual recognition of an abstraction beneath the surface of the language. The "teeth" are admired as they function "cutting off men from their errors," and the "shorn sheep" are pleasantly, but intellectually, envisaged as "those who have put aside the burdens of the world like so much fleece." The passage from the Canticle is seen to conform, as it were, to the abstract pattern of behavior expected of holy men, and the discovery of this abstract pattern is experienced as a pleasing intellectual revelation. Much of the figurative material in medieval writing, and, in fact, much of the symbolism in medieval art, was designed to have exactly this kind of appeal; the function of figurative expression was not to arouse spontaneous emotional attitudes based on the personal experience of the observer, but to encourage the observer to seek an abstract pattern of philosophical significance beneath the symbolic configuration. In this respect, as in other respects, medieval art is considerably more objective than modern art, even in those instances where it is least "realistic." [8] Its referents were characteristically not elements in the emotional life of the artist or the observer, but abstract ideas forming a part of a philosophical tradition independent of either the artist or the observer. Neither St. Augustine nor his medieval followers expected the meaning to emerge from either a verbal or a vis-

[8] Cf. the observations of Otto von Simson, *The Gothic Cathedral* (New York, 1956), pp. xix ff.

ual figurative construction "in the likeness of one of those misty halos that sometimes are made visible by the special illumination of moonshine."

The obscurity of Scripture, then, was happily arranged, since "no one doubts that things are perceived more readily through similitudes and that what is sought with difficulty is discovered with more pleasure." The same idea is repeated with some elaboration in 4. 8. 22, where it is said that some things in the Scriptures "have been spoken with a useful and healthful obscurity for the purpose of exercising and sharpening, as it were, the minds of the readers and of destroying fastidiousness and stimulating the desire to learn, concealing their intention in such a way that the minds of the impious are either converted to piety or excluded from the mysteries of the faith." In one of his letters (LV), Augustine adds that this process of exercise and discovery leads to love for the abstractions shadowed by the temporal things used to form the figurative language.

It is not surprising that the same arguments were used by later writers to account for the obscurity of poetry and to defend it against those who, like St. Thomas Aquinas,[9] maintained that the figurative language of poetry has no utility. Petrarch, for example, quotes St. Augustine and St. Gregory on the function of scriptural obscurity and adds: "If these things are said truly concerning those writings which are set before all readers, how much more truly may they be said of writings intended for a few! Among poets . . . a majesty and dignity of style are maintained, not so that those who are worthy may be prevented from understanding, but so that, a sweet labor having been presented to them, they may be benefited at once in memory and delight; for those things which we seek with difficulty are dearer to us and more carefully heeded. And for those who are unworthy it is provided that, lest they exhaust themselves in vain on the surfaces of these things, if they are wise, they are discouraged from approaching them." [10]

9 Cf. *Summa theol.* 1. 1. 9; 1-2. 101. 2 ad 2.
10 *Invective*, ed. Ricci, pp. 69-70.

The Augustinian notion of exercise followed by pleasing discovery was Petrarch's favorite critical principle. To dismiss the notion itself as a mere indication of the "decadence" of late antiquity, as some have done, requires that we extend that decadence for a rather considerable period. Late medieval defenders of poetry were almost as bitter about those who failed to understand the spirit beneath the letter as St. Augustine was about those similarly recalcitrant in scriptural study (3. 5. 9). Boccaccio urges them, in fact, to "put off the old mind, and put on the new and noble," [11] implying that if a spiritual mind is necessary to read the Scriptures, it is also necessary to read poetry. And Salutati, in a long letter to Iohannes Dominici, explains at length that the allegorical character of poetry is like the allegorical character of the Bible, all of which, he says, is "mystical" and capable of being reduced to an "allegorical understanding." Among other things, he advises this "Thomistic" enemy of poetry to "read and consider the most holy and learned books of the divine Augustine, whose title is *On Christian Doctrine.*" There he should learn that "all the holy Scriptures overflow in spiritual senses and abound everywhere in various divine mysteries; and this," Salutati adds, "is the special excellence of poets." [12] It is not difficult to detect the influence of *On Christian Doctrine* in many of the statements about poetry which survive from the twelfth century to the Renaissance, and the pattern of St. Augustine's conception of symbolic imagery is still recognizable in Cardinal Paleotti's defense of painting (1582).

The rhetorical principles which St. Augustine adduces as a guide to the exposition of Scripture in Book IV are not without historical interest, especially since he shows none of the servile respect for rules which was characteristic of some of his contemporaries. Cicero had emphasized the idea that the mere study of rules is insufficient for the education of the orator; St. Augustine goes further, maintaining that the rules are not necessary at all. It is sufficient for the wise man who

[11] C. G. Osgood, *Boccaccio on Poetry* (New York, 1956), p. 61.
[12] *Epist.*, ed. Novati, IV, pp. 238-239.

wishes also to be eloquent to study the masters of Christian
eloquence and, above all, the Bible, which, as he is at some
pains to show, is not without eloquence itself. It has, in fact,
an eloquence of its own different from but not inferior to that
of pagan writers. Since much of what St. Augustine· says in
Book IV is based on Cicero, it may be useful here to review
very briefly the systematic principles of Ciceronian rhetoric.

For the preparation of a speech, the orator concerned himself with five separate tasks: (1) *inventio,* the collection of materials; (2) *dispositio,* the arrangement of the materials; (3)
elocutio, the verbal expression of the materials; (4) *memoria,*
the memorization of the speech; (5) *actio,* the technique of delivery. Each of these tasks was regulated by a series of subsidi-
ary considerations. Thus under *inventio* the orator would consider *loci communes,* or "topics." Under *dispositio* he would
take into account the conventional parts of the oration: *ex-
ordium, narratio, confutatio, refutatio, peroratio.* And, in the
same way, there were systematic procedures governing the
other tasks of the orator. The speech as a whole would be set
predominantly, but usually not exclusively, in one of the three
styles: plain, moderate, and grand. This stylistic distinction
probably had its origin in a distinction made by Theophras-
tus between two kinds of language: (1) an unadorned language
suited to factual statement or argument, and (2) a more orna-
mental language suited to the expression of emotion. This implied a difference between "dialectical" and "rhetorical" modes
of expression which came to be known as the "plain" and the
"grand" styles. The third or "moderate" style seems to have
been added as a mean between the two extremes. The plain
style was used for instruction or proof. Either might be rather
complex, so that the plain or "subdued" style is not necessarily
simple. Again, reasoning developed in the plain style may be
rhetorically very effective. The moderate style, more ornamented than the plain but less overpowering than the grand,
was thought of as a pleasing style. And the grand style was
used to move the audience. However, these were not rigid
categories; there might, for example, be many intermediate

stages between a severely plain style and a clearly moderate style. Moreover, the orator was expected to vary the styles during the course of a single oration. It is noteworthy, finally, that these styles are not altogether a matter of the text of the oration itself; the manner of delivery may affect them.

St. Augustine refuses to supply his readers with a set of rhetorical rules, but he does call attention to certain ornaments of speech which are found in the Bible as well as in the works of pagan authors. In particular, he shows the effective use of *caesa, membra,* and the *circuitus* in scriptural texts. It should be emphasized that these terms are primarily descriptive of oral effects rather than of written texts, so that although a written text does limit the possibilities of their application, it is sometimes susceptible to two or more oral interpretations. There are, furthermore, no exact equivalents for these terms in English, and their precise meanings in Latin are not always clear. However, if we follow Quintilian, a *caesum,* or, as he calls it, an *incisum,* is an expression which contains a complete meaning but is pronounced with an incomplete rhythm, that is, with the rhythm suspended as though something is to follow. A *membrum* contains a complete meaning and a complete rhythm, but the meaning is not complete when it is considered in relation to the sentence as a whole. In these definitions "a complete meaning" does not mean what English grammars call "a complete thought"; rather it indicates a unit of discourse which may be followed by a pause. In a *circuitus* or "period" consisting of a series of two or more *membra,* the rhythm is suspended at the close of each *membrum* except the last. In considering St. Augustine's application of these concepts in Book IV, the reader should bear in mind the fact that English inflection and syntax do not reflect Latin inflection and syntax with sufficient accuracy so that the translated examples can afford no more than a very crude approximation of the original.

Throughout the discussion of oratory St. Augustine emphasizes the special qualities of Christian as opposed to pagan eloquence. Instead of replying to the charge that the Scriptures are inferior in style as Minucius Felix had done in the *Octavius*—*non loquimur magna sed vivimus,* "we do not speak great things, but live them"—St. Augustine sets out to show that the Scriptures have an eloquence exactly suited to the peculiar position of their authors and the gravity of the subject they treat. This eloquence should be imitated by the expositor, except that his discourse should not reflect the obscurity of the Bible; he should at all times be clear. He should not be concerned to win applause for himself, and hence his use of the moderate style will be different from that of his pagan contemporaries. He should seek to teach, to please, and to move at all times. If he cannot speak eloquently, he should speak wisely; and if he lives well, there may be a kind of persuasive eloquence in his life.

A few bibliographical references may be helpful. A convenient general introduction to St. Augustine's life and work is Roy W. Battenhouse (ed.), *A Companion to St. Augustine* (New York, 1955). A brief but stimulating general work which contains many interesting illustrations and some selections from St. Augustine's writings is Henri Marrou, *Saint Augustin et l'augustinisme* (Paris, 1956), now available also in English in the "Men of Wisdom" series (New York and London, 1957). The edition and translation of the *De doctrina christiana* in the volume of the "Bibliothèque Augustinienne" entitled *Le magistère chrétien* (Paris, 1949) by G. Combès and J. Farges contains notes and references. There is an annotated edition and translation of Book IV by Sister Thérèse Sullivan (Washington, D. C., 1930) which should be consulted by all those interested in rhetoric. A series of translations from the works of St. Augustine generally is available in the volumes called *Basic Writings of St. Augustine,* edited by Whitney J. Oates (New York, 1948). By far the best account of the place of *On Christian Doctrine* in the culture of its time is H. I. Marrou, *Saint Augustin et la fin de la culture antique* (Paris, 1938). For the influence of St. Augustine in the preservation of classical culture, there is a good essay by Martin Grabmann, "Der Einfluss des heiligen Augustinus auf die Verwertung und Bewertung der Antike im Mittelalter," in *Mittelalterliches Geistesleben,* II (Munich, 1936), 1-24. St. Augustine's statements relevant to aesthetic matters are carefully collected and discussed by K. Svoboda, *L'esthétique de Saint Augustin* (Brno, 1933). The best introduction to the theory of poetic allegory in the Middle Ages is C. G. Osgood, *Boccaccio on Poetry,* now available in "The Library of Liberal Arts."

D. W. ROBERTSON, JR.

SELECTED BIBLIOGRAPHY

A. GUIDES

Altaner, B. *Patrologie.* 2 ed., 1950.

O'Meara, J. J. "The Works of St. Augustine and a Bibliographical Guide." In Henri Marrou. *Saint Augustine.* "Harper Torchbooks," New York, 1957. Contains a convenient list of St. Augustine's works with indications showing where both Latin texts and English translations may be found.

B. WORKS (LATIN)

Opera omnia. Edited by the Benedictines of St. Maur. Published separately, Paris, 1836-1838. Also in J. P. Migne, *Patrologiae cursus completus, series latina,* Vols. XXXII-XLVI. Paris, 1841-1842. This text with occasional modifications, together with French translations, is being published in the *Bibliothèque Augustinienne,* Paris. More modern texts have appeared in two other series: *Corpus scriptorum ecclesiasticorum latinorum* and *Corpus christianorum.*

C. Works (English)

A Select Library of the Nicene and Post-Nicene Fathers. Buffalo, 1886. The translations included here had appeared elsewhere in earlier series. More recent translations of some works appear in current series like "Ancient Christian Writers," Westminster, Maryland; "The Fathers of the Church," New York; "The Library of Christian Classics," Philadelphia. A convenient and representative selection has been edited by Whitney J. Oates: *Basic Writings of St. Augustine.* New York, 1948.

D. Studies

Battenhouse, R. W. et al. *A Companion to the Study of St. Augustine.* New York, 1954.

D'Arcy, M. C. et al. *A Monument to St. Augustine.* London, 1930.

Finaert, G. *Saint Augustin rhéteur.* Paris, 1939.

Gilson, E. *Introduction à l'étude de saint Augustin.* 2 ed. Paris, 1943.

Marrou, H. I. *Saint Augustin et la fin de la culture antique.* 2 ed. Paris, 1949.

O'Meara, J. J. *The Young Augustine.* London, 1945.

Pontet, M. *L'exégèse de saint Augustin prédicateur.* Paris, 1946.

Przywara, E. *An Augustinian Synthesis.* New York, 1936.

ON CHRISTIAN DOCTRINE

PROLOGUE

1. There are certain precepts for treating the Scriptures which I think may not inconveniently be transmitted to students, so that they may profit not only from reading the work of expositors but also in their own explanations of the sacred writings to others. I have undertaken to explain these rules to those able and willing to learn, if God our Lord will not deny me, in writing, those things which He usually suggests to me in thought. But before I begin this task, it seems proper to answer those who will condemn these precepts, or who would condemn them if we did not placate them beforehand. If some condemn them anyhow, at least they will not influence others, nor call them from useful study to vain idleness, as they might have been able to do if they had not found them already armed and prepared.

2. Some will condemn our work because they do not understand the precepts it contains. Others, however, when they have understood our rules and wish to use them and have sought to treat the Sacred Scriptures in accordance with them but have been unable to clarify and explain what they wish, will judge that I have labored in vain. And since this work has not helped them, they will decide that it can help no one. There are detractors of a third type who either treat the Sacred Scriptures well, or think they do. These see, or think they see, that they are already equipped to expound the sacred books without having read any of the observations which I have set out to make, so that they will declare that these regulations are necessary to no one, but that everything which may laudably be revealed about the obscurities of those books can be revealed with divine assistance.

3. Answering all these objections briefly, to those who do not understand what we write, I say this: I am not to blame because they do not understand. In the same way, if they

wished to see the old or the new moon or some very small star which I was pointing to with my finger and they did not have keen enough sight even to see my finger, they should not on that account become angry with me. And those who have studied and learned these precepts and still do not understand the obscurities of the Holy Scriptures think that they can see my finger but not the heavenly bodies which it was intended to point out. But both of these groups should stop blaming me and ask God to give them vision. Although I can lift my finger to point something out, I cannot supply the vision by means of which either this gesture or what it indicates can be seen.

4. Moreover, those who exult in divine assistance and who glory in being able to understand and to treat the sacred books without precepts of the kind which I have undertaken to supply herewith, so that they think these precepts superfluous, should calm themselves for this reason: although they may rightfully rejoice in the great gift God has given them, they should remember that they have learned at least the alphabet from men. Nor should they for this reason feel themselves injured by Antony, the holy and perfect Egyptian monk, who is said to have memorized the Sacred Scriptures simply by hearing them, without any training in reading, and to have understood them through prudent thinking. Nor should they be offended by that foreign Christian slave, about whom we have recently heard from serious and reliable people, who, although no one had taught him to read, prayed that the skill might be revealed to him, and after three days of prayer read a book which was handed to him, to the astonishment of those who were present.

5. If anyone thinks these stories to be false, I shall not take up arms. Indeed, since our concern is with Christians who rejoice to know the Sacred Scriptures without human instruction —and if they do know them in this way they do not rejoice in a mediocre gift—it is necessary that they concede that any one of us has learned his own language by hearing it spoken habitually from childhood, and any other language such as

Greek or Hebrew or the like either by hearing it or by human instruction. Now, should we admonish all of our brethren not to teach these things to their children because the apostles, filled in a single moment with the Holy Spirit, spoke in the languages of all peoples? [1] Or, when such things do not come to anyone, are we to conclude that he is not a Christian or that he has not received the Holy Spirit? Rather, those things which can be learned from men should be learned without pride. And let anyone teaching another communicate what he has received [2] without pride or envy. We should not tempt Him in whom we have believed, lest, deceived by the wiles and perversity of the Enemy, we should be unwilling to go to church to hear and learn the Gospels, or to read a book, or to hear a man reading or teaching, but expect to be "caught up to the third heaven," as the Apostle says, "whether in the body or out of the body," and there hear "secret words that man may not repeat," [3] or there see Our Lord Jesus Christ and hear the gospel from Him rather than from men.

6. We should beware of most proud and most dangerous temptations of this kind and think rather that the Apostle Paul himself, although prostrated and taught by the divine and heavenly voice, was nevertheless sent to a man that he might receive the sacraments and be joined to the church. [4] And the centurion Cornelius, although an angel announced to him that his prayers had been heard and his alms recognized, was sent to Peter for instruction. He not only received the sacraments from him, but was also taught what should be believed, what should be hoped, and what should be loved. [5] And all of these things in both instances might have been done by an angel, but the condition of man would be lowered if God had not wished to have men supply His word to men. How would there be truth in what is said—"For the temple of God is holy, which you are" [6]—if God did not give responses from a human temple, but called out all that He wished to be

[1] Acts 2. 1-11.
[2] Wisd. 7. 13; 1 Cor. 11. 23.
[3] 2 Cor. 12. 2, 4.
[4] Acts 9. 3-18.
[5] Acts 10.
[6] 1 Cor. 3. 17.

taught to men from Heaven and through angels? For charity itself, which holds men together in a knot of unity, would not have a means of infusing souls and almost mixing them together if men could teach nothing to men.

7. And surely the Apostle did not send the eunuch who did not understand what he read in the prophet Isaias to an angel, nor was what he did not understand either explained to him by an angel or revealed to him divinely in his mind without human ministration. Rather Philip, who understood the prophet Isaias, was sent to him by divine suggestion, sat with him, and explained to him what was hidden in that Scripture in human words and discourse.[7] Did not God speak to Moses? And yet did he not accept counsel concerning the government and administration of a great nation from his father-in-law, although he was a stranger, in a most provident and humble way? [8] For Moses knew that, from whatever mind true counsel might proceed, it should not be attributed to that mind but to Him who is the truth, immutable God.

8. Finally, whoever, instructed by no precepts, glories in his understanding of whatever is obscure in the Scriptures through a divine gift, believes correctly in thinking that his ability does not come from himself but is divinely given, so that he seeks the glory of God and not his own. But when he reads and understands without the explanations of men, why does he presume to explain to others? Why does he not rather send them to God that they also may be inwardly instructed, not by men but by Him? Obviously, he may fear lest he hear from the Lord, "Wicked servant . . . thou oughtest therefore to have committed my money to the bankers." [9] Just as they, in so far as they understand, teach others in speaking or writing, so also, if I should teach not only what they understand but in addition those things which are to be observed in understanding, I certainly should not be condemned by them. For no one should consider anything his own, except perhaps a lie, since all truth is from Him who said, "I am the truth." [10]

7 Acts 8. 27-35.
8 Exod. 18. 14-27.
9 Matt. 25. 26-27.
10 John 14. 6.

For what have we which we have not received? And if we have received, why do we glory as if we had not received it? [11]

9. He who reads to others pronounces the words he recognizes; he who teaches reading does so that others may also read; but both make known what they receive. In the same way, he who explains to listeners what he understands in the Scriptures is like a reader who pronounces the words he knows, but he who teaches how the Scriptures are to be understood is like a teacher who advises how the words are to be read. Just as a man who knows how to read will not need another reader from whom he may hear what is written when he finds a book, he who receives the precepts we wish to teach will not need another to reveal those things which need explaining when he finds any obscurity in books, since he has certain rules like those used in reading in his understanding. But by following certain traces he may come to the hidden sense without any error, or at least he will not fall into the absurdity of wicked meanings. Therefore, although in this work itself it may be sufficiently clear that no one ought to criticize our labors, nevertheless, if a prologue such as this may be seen as a convenient response to objectors, it seemed to us a proper beginning for the road we wished to follow.

BOOK ONE

I

1. There are two things necessary to the treatment of the Scriptures: a way of discovering those things which are to be understood, and a way of teaching what we have learned. We shall speak first of discovery and second of teaching. This is a great and arduous work, and since it is difficult to sustain, I fear some temerity in undertaking it. It would be thus indeed if I relied on myself alone, but now while the hope of com-

[11] Cf. 1 Cor. 4. 7.

pleting such a work lies in Him from whom I have received
much concerning these things in thought, it is not to be feared
that He will cease giving me more when I have begun to use
what He has already given me. Everything which does not
decrease on being given away is not properly owned when it is
owned and not given. For He says, "He that hath, to him shall
be given." [1] Therefore He will give to those that have, that is,
to those benevolently using that which they have received He
will increase and heap up what He gives. There were at one
time five loaves and at another time seven before they began
to be given to the needy; [2] and when this began to be done,
baskets and hampers were filled, although thousands of men
were fed. Just as the loaves increased when they were broken,
the Lord has granted those things necessary to the beginning
of this work, and when they begin to be given out they will be
multiplied by His inspiration, so that in this task of mine I
shall not only suffer no poverty of ideas but shall rejoice in
wonderful abundance.

II

2. All doctrine concerns either things or signs, but things
are learned by signs. Strictly speaking, I have here called a
"thing" that which is not used to signify something else, like
wood, stone, cattle, and so on; but not that wood concerning
which we read that Moses cast it into bitter waters that their
bitterness might be dispelled, [3] nor that stone which Jacob
placed at his head, [4] nor that beast which Abraham sacrificed
in place of his son. [5] For these are things in such a way that
they are also signs of other things. [6] There are other signs
whose whole use is in signifying, like words. For no one uses
words except for the purpose of signifying something. From
this may be understood what we call "signs"; they are things

---

[1] Matt. 13. 12.   [4] Gen. 28. 11.
[2] Matt. 14. 17; 15. 34.   [5] Gen. 22. 13.
[3] Exod. 15. 25.

[6] According to St. Augustine, the "wood" is a sign of the cross. The
"stone" and the "beast" represent the human nature of Christ.

used to signify something. Thus every sign is also a thing, for that which is not a thing is nothing at all; but not every thing is also a sign. And thus in this distinction between things and signs, when we speak of things, we shall so speak that, although some of them may be used to signify something else, this fact shall not disturb the arrangement we have made to speak of things as such first and of signs later. We should bear in mind that now we are to consider what things are, not what they signify beyond themselves.

things exist prior to signs

III

3. Some things are to be enjoyed, others to be used, and there are others which are to be enjoyed and used. Those things which are to be enjoyed make us blessed. Those things which are to be used help and, as it were, sustain us as we move toward blessedness in order that we may gain and cling to those things which make us blessed. If we who enjoy and use things, being placed in the midst of things of both kinds, wish to enjoy those things which should be used, our course will be impeded and sometimes deflected, so that we are retarded in obtaining those things which are to be enjoyed, or even prevented altogether, shackled by an inferior love.

IV

4. To enjoy something is to cling to it with love for its own sake. To use something, however, is to employ it in obtaining that which you love, provided that it is worthy of love. For an illicit use should be called rather a waste or an abuse. Suppose we were wanderers who could not live in blessedness except at home, miserable in our wandering and desiring to end it and to return to our native country. We would need vehicles for land and sea which could be used to help us to reach our homeland, which is to be enjoyed. But if the amenities of the journey and the motion of the vehicles itself delighted us, and we were led to enjoy those things which we should use, we should not wish to end our journey quickly, and, entangled in

a perverse sweetness, we should be alienated from our country, whose' sweetness would make us blessed. Thus in this
mortal life, wandering from God,[1] if we wish to return to our
native country where we can be blessed we should use this
world and not enjoy it, so that the "invisible things" of God
"being understood by the things that are made" [2] may be seen,
that is, so that by means of corporal and temporal things we
may comprehend the eternal and spiritual.

V

5. The things which are to be enjoyed are the Father, the
Son, and the Holy Spirit, a single Trinity, a certain supreme
thing common to all who enjoy it, if, indeed, it is a thing and
not rather the cause of all things, or both a thing and a cause.
It is not easy to find a name proper to such excellence, unless
it is better to say that this Trinity is one God and that "of
him, and by him, and in him are all things." [1] Thus there are
the Father, the Son, and the Holy Spirit, and each is God, and
at the same time all are one God; and each of them is a full
substance, and at the same time all are one substance. The
Father is neither the Son nor the Holy Spirit; the Son is
neither the Father nor the Holy Spirit; the Holy Spirit is
neither the Father nor the Son. But the Father is the Father
uniquely; the Son is the Son uniquely; and the Holy Spirit is
the Holy Spirit uniquely. All three have the same eternity, the
same immutability, the same majesty, and the same power. In
the Father is unity, in the Son equality, and in the Holy
Spirit a concord of unity and equality; and these three qualities are all one because of the Father, all equal because of the
Son, and all united because of the Holy Spirit.

VI

6. Have we spoken or announced anything worthy of God?
Rather I feel that I have done nothing but wish to speak: if I

[1] Cf. 2 Cor. 5. 6 (Vulg.).   [2] Rom. 1. 20.   [1] Rom. 11. 36.

have spoken, I have not said what I wished to say. Whence do I know this, except because God is ineffable? If what I said were ineffable, it would not be said. And for this reason God should not be said to be ineffable, for when this is said something is said. And a contradiction in terms is created, since if that is ineffable which cannot be spoken, then that is not ineffable which can be called ineffable. This contradiction is to be passed over in silence rather than resolved verbally. For God, although nothing worthy may be spoken of Him, has accepted the tribute of the human voice and wished us to take joy in praising Him with our words. In this way he is called *Deus*. Although He is not recognized in the noise of these two syllables, all those who know the Latin language, when this sound reaches their ears, are moved to think of a certain most excellent immortal nature.

VII

7. For when the one God of gods is thought of, even by those who recognize, invoke, and worship other gods either in Heaven or on earth, He is thought of in such a way that the thought seeks to attain something than which there is nothing better or more sublime. Since men are moved by diverse goods, some by those which appeal to the bodily senses, some by those which pertain to the understanding of the mind, those who are given to the bodily senses think the God of gods to be either the sky, or that which they see shining most brightly in the sky, or the world itself. Or, if they seek to go beyond the world, they imagine something luminous or infinite, or with a vain notion shape it in that form which seems best to them, perhaps thinking of the form of the human body if they place that above others. If they do not think of a God of gods but rather of innumerable gods of equal rank, they shape them in their minds according to that bodily shape which they think excellent. Those, however, who seek to know what God is through the understanding place Him above all things mutable, either visible and corporal or intelligible and spiritual. All men struggle emulously for the excellence of God, and no

one can be found who believes God to be something to which
there is a superior. Thus all agree that God is that thing which
they place above all other things.

VIII

8. And since all those who think of God think of something
living, only they can think of Him without absurdity who
think of Him as life itself. For whatever bodily form may
occur to them, they think of it as either vivified by life or not
living, and they value that which is vivified by life above the
not living. And they understand that the living form of the
body, however it may excel in radiance, size, or beauty, is
different from the life which vivifies it, and they consider this
life to have a dignity incomparable with that of the mass it
animates. Then they come to think of life itself, and if they
find it insentient, as in trees, they place the sentient life of
animals above it, and they value even more highly the intelligent life of men. But when they find this to be mutable, they
are forced to value still more highly an immutable life, a life
which is not sometimes foolish and sometimes wise but is
rather Wisdom itself. For a wise mind which has learned
wisdom was not wise before it learned it, but Wisdom itself
was never foolish and never can be. If men did not see this,
they would not confidently place an immutably wise life above
a mutable one. For they see that this rule of truth by which
they hold immutable wisdom to be better is itself immutable,
nor can they see it anywhere except above their own nature,
for they are themselves mutable.

IX

9. No one is so impudently stupid as to say, "How do you
know that an immutable wise life is preferable to a mutable
one?" For the thing he asks—whence I know—is commonly and
unchangeably obvious to all who think about it. And he who
does not see it is like a blind man in the sun who profits nothing when his eyesockets are infused with the brilliance of the

clear and immediate light. But he who sees the truth and flees has weakened the acuteness of his mind through the habit of carnal shadows. For men are driven back from their country by evil habits as by contrary breezes, seeking things farther back from and inferior to that which they confess to be better and more worthy.

X

10. Therefore, since that truth is to be enjoyed which lives immutably, and since God the Trinity, the Author and Founder of the universe, cares for His creatures through that truth, the mind should be cleansed so that it is able to see that light and to cling to it once it is seen. Let us consider this cleansing to be as a journey or voyage home. But we do not come to Him who is everywhere present by moving from place to place, but by good endeavor and good habits.

XI

11. We would not be able to do this except that Wisdom Himself saw fit to make Himself congruous with such infirmity as ours and to set an example of living for us, not otherwise than as a man, since we ourselves are men. Since we do wisely when we come to Him, He was thought by proud men to do foolishly when He came to us. And since when we come to Him we grow strong, He was thought to be weak when He came to us. But "the foolishness of God is wiser than men; and the weakness of God is stronger than men." [1] Although He is our native country, He made Himself also the Way to that country.[2]

XII

Although to the healthy and pure internal eye He is every-where present, He saw fit to appear to those whose eye is weak and impure, and even to fleshly eyes. "For seeing that in the wisdom of God the world, by wisdom, knew not God, it

[1] 1 Cor. 1. 25.   [2] Cf. John 14. 6.

pleased God, by the foolishness of preaching, to save them that believe." [1]

12. Thus He is said to have come to us, not from place to place through space, but by appearing to mortals in mortal flesh. He came to a place where He was already, for He was in the world, and the world was made by Him. But since men were made conformable to this world by a desire to enjoy creatures instead of their creator, whence they are most aptly called "the world," they did not know Him, so that the Evangelist says, "the world knew Him not." [2] Thus in the Wisdom of God the world could not know God through wisdom. Why did He come when He was already here unless "it pleased God, by the foolishness of preaching, to save them that believe"?

XIII

How did He come except that "the Word was made flesh, and dwelt among us"? [1] It is as when we speak. In order that what we are thinking may reach the mind of the listener through the fleshly ears, that which we have in mind is expressed in words and is called speech. But our thought is not transformed into sounds; it remains entire in itself and assumes the form of words by means of which it may reach the ears without suffering any deterioration in itself. In the same way the Word of God was made flesh without change that He might dwell among us.

XIV

13. Just as a cure is the way to health, so also this Cure received sinners to heal and strengthen them. And just as physicians when they bind up wounds do not do so haphazardly but neatly so that a certain beauty accompanies the utility of the bandages, so the medicine of Wisdom by taking on humanity is accommodated to our wounds, healing some by contraries

[1] 1 Cor. 1. 21.   [2] John 1. 10.   [1] John 1. 14.

and some by similar things. He who tends the wounds of the body sometimes applies contraries, such as cold to hot, moist to dry, and so on; at other times he applies similar things, like a round bandage for a round wound or an oblong bandage for an oblong wound, not using the same bandage for all members but fitting similar things to similar. Thus the Wisdom of God, setting out to cure men, applied Himself to cure them, being at once the Physician and the Medicine. Because man fell through pride, He applied humility as a cure. We were trapped by the wisdom of the serpent; we are freed by the foolishness of God. Just as that which was called wisdom was foolishness in those who condemned God, thus this which is called foolishness is wisdom in those who conquer the Devil. We ill used our immortality, so that we deserved to die; Christ used His mortality well to restore us. Our malady arose through the corrupted spirit of a woman; from the incorrupted flesh of a woman proceeded our salvation. The same principle of contraries is illustrated in the fact that the example of His virtues cures our vices. But the following things are like similar bandages applied to our wounds and members: that, born of a woman, He freed those deceived by a woman; that as a man He freed men; that as a mortal He freed mortals; that in death He freed the dead. Instruction will reveal many other examples of Christian medicine operating either by contraries or by similar things to those who diligently consider and are not hurried away by the necessity of completing some task they have begun.

XV

14. Indeed, the belief in the Resurrection of Our Lord from death, and in His Ascension into Heaven, has strengthened our faith with great hope. For this shows very clearly how He was willing to give His life for ours when He had power to take it up again.[1] With what great trust is the hope of the faithful strengthened when they consider that such a man suffered so

---

[1] Cf. John 10. 18.

much for those who did not yet believe! When He is expected as the Judge of the living and the dead from Heaven, the thought strikes great fear into the negligent, so that they turn to loving Him and prefer to desire Him in doing well than to fear Him in doing evil. With what words may we describe or with what thoughts conceive the reward which He will give in the end, when He has given so much of His spirit as a consolation in this journey to the end that in the adversities of this life we may have great faith and love for Him whom we have never seen? Again, He has given to each gifts proper to the building of His Church so that what He showed that we should do we may do, not only without murmuring, but also with delight.

XVI

15. For the Church "is His body," [1] as apostolic teaching asserts, and it is also called His bride. Therefore He binds His body, which has many members performing diverse offices, in a bond of unity and charity which is, as it were, its health. He exercises it in this world and cleanses it with certain medicinal adversities, so that when it is delivered from the world He may join Himself in eternity with His bride, the Church, "not having spot or wrinkle, or any such thing." [2]

XVII

16. Moreover, since we are on a road which is not a road from place to place but a road of the affections, which was blocked, as if by a thorny hedge, by the malice of our past sins, what more liberal and merciful thing could He do when He wished to lay down Himself as a means for our return than to forgive all our sins, after we turn to Him, and to tear away the firmly fixed prohibitions preventing our return by being crucified for us?

[1] Eph. 1. 23.   [2] Cf. Eph. 5. 23-27.

XVIII

17. He gave, therefore, the keys to His Church, so that what-soever it should loose on earth might be loosed in Heaven and that whatsoever it should bind on earth should be bound in Heaven.[1] That is, He did this so that whoever in His Church did not believe his sins to be forgiven should not have them forgiven, but whoever believed and in correction turned him-self from them, having placed himself in the bosom of His Church, should be healed by that faith and correction. And whoever does not believe that his sins can be forgiven worsens in desperation, as if nothing better than evil remained to him since he has no faith in the fruits of his conversion.

XIX

18. Just as there is a certain death of the soul in the aban-donment of former life and habits which is made through penance, so also the death of the body marks the resolution of the principle which first animated it. And just as the soul after penance, by means of which it puts aside its former evil habits, is reformed for the better, so also the body, after the death we all owe because of the bond of sin, will, we must believe and hope, be changed for the better at the time of resurrection, not so that flesh and blood may possess the King-dom of Heaven, for that is impossible, but so that "this cor-ruptible must put on incorruption, and this mortal must put on immortality." [2] Then the body will cause no trouble be-cause it will not suffer want; it will be animated by a blessed and perfected soul in the utmost peace.

XX

19. But the soul of one who neither dies to this world nor begins to conform himself to truth is drawn by the death of

[1] Cf. Matt. 16. 19.   [2] 1 Cor. 15. 53.

the body into a more serious death; he will revive, not to the transformation of a celestial dwelling, but to a subjection to torments.

XXI

This faith maintains, and it must be believed: neither the soul nor the human body may suffer complete annihilation, but the impious shall rise again into everlasting punishment, and the just into life everlasting.[1]

XXII

20. Therefore, among all these things only those are to be enjoyed which we have described as being eternal and immutable; others are to be used so that we may be able to enjoy those. In the same way we who enjoy and use other things are things ourselves. A great thing is man, made in the image and likeness of God,[2] not in that he is encased in a mortal body, but in that he excels the beasts in the dignity of a rational soul. Thus there is a profound question as to whether men should enjoy themselves, use themselves, or do both. For it is commanded to us that we should love one another,[3] but it is to be asked whether man is to be loved by man for his own sake or for the sake of something else. If for his own sake, we enjoy him; if for the sake of something else, we use him. But I think that man is to be loved for the sake of something else. In that which is to be loved for its own sake the blessed life resides; and if we do not have it for the present, the hope for it now consoles us. But "cursed be the man that trusteth in man." [4]

21. But no one ought to enjoy himself either, if you observe the matter closely, because he should not love himself on account of himself but on account of Him who is to be enjoyed. For he is the best man who turns his whole life toward the immutable life and adheres to it with all his affection. But if

---

1 Cf. Matt. 25. 46.   3 Cf. John 15. 12.
2 Cf. Gen. 1. 26.   4 Jer. 17. 5.

he loves himself on his own account he does not turn himself toward God, but, being turned toward himself, he does not care for anything immutable. Therefore his enjoyment of himself is imperfect, for he is better when he adheres to and is bound completely to the immutable good than when he lapses away from it, even toward himself. If, therefore, you should love yourself not on your own account but on account of Him who is most justly the object of your love, no other man should feel angry with you if you love him also on account of God. This is the divinely instituted rule of love: "Thou shalt love thy neighbor as thyself," He said, and "Thou shalt love God with thy whole heart, and with thy whole soul, and with thy whole mind." [5] Thus all your thoughts and all your life and all your understanding should be turned toward Him from whom you receive these powers. For when He said, "With thy whole heart, and with thy whole soul, and with thy whole mind," He did not leave any part of life which should be free and find itself room to desire the enjoyment of something else. But whatever else appeals to the mind as being lovable should be directed into that channel into which the whole current of love flows. Whoever, therefore, justly loves his neighbor should so act toward him that he also loves God with his whole heart, with his whole soul, and with his whole mind. Thus, loving his neighbor as himself, he refers the love of both to that love of God which suffers no stream to be led away from it by which it might be diminished.

XXIII

22. Not everything which is to be used is to be loved, but only those things which either by a certain association pertain to God, like a man or an angel, or pertain to us and require the favor of God through us, like the body. For undoubtedly the martyrs did not love the evil of those who persecuted them, even though they used it to merit God. Although there are four kinds of things which may be loved—first, the kind which

[5] Lev. 19. 18; Deut. 6. 5; Matt. 22. 39, 37.

is above us; second, the kind which constitutes ourselves; third, the kind which is equal to us; and fourth, the kind which is below us—no precepts need to be given concerning the second and the fourth. However much a man departs from the truth, there remains in him the love of himself and of his body. For the spirit, having fled from the immutable light which reigns over all, acts so that it may rule itself and its own body, and thus cannot do otherwise than love itself and its own body.

23. Moreover, it thinks it has gained much when it can also rule over its associates, who are other men. For it is the nature of the vicious spirit to desire greatly and to claim as its desert that which is properly due only to God. Such self-love is better called hate. For it is iniquitous for the spirit to wish those below it to serve it and to refuse at the same time to serve a superior, and it is said most justly, "He that loveth iniquity hateth his own soul." [1] And in this way the soul is made weak and tortured by the mortal body. It is forced to love the body and is weighted down by its corruption. For immortality and purity of the body arise from the health of the spirit, and the health of the spirit arises from a firm adherence to something more powerful, that is, to immutable God. When it endeavors to dominate those who are naturally its peers, other men, its pride is altogether intolerable.

XXIV

24. Thus no one hates himself. And, indeed, this principle was never questioned by any sect. Neither does anyone hate his body, and what the Apostle says concerning this is true: "No man ever hated his own flesh." [2] And that which some say, that they would rather be without a body, arises from a complete delusion: they hate not their bodies but the corruption and solidity of their bodies. They do not wish to have no bodies at all but rather incorruptible and most agile bodies, and they think that no body could be so constituted because then it would be a spirit. Those who seem to perse-

[1] Ps. 10. 5 [11. 5].   [2] Eph. 5. 29.

cute their bodies with continence and labors, if they do so correctly, do not act so that they may not have bodies but so that their bodies may be subjugated and prepared for necessary work. They seek to extinguish those desires which misuse the body, or those habits and inclinations of the spirit toward the enjoyment of inferior things, by a certain laborious warfare on the part of the body itself. But they do not strive to destroy themselves; on the contrary, they show care for their own health.

25. Those who seek to do this perversely war on their bodies as though they were natural enemies. In this way they have been deceived by the words, "The flesh lusteth against the spirit: and the spirit against the flesh; for these are contrary to one another." [1] For this was said on account of the unconquered habit of the flesh against which the spirit has a concupiscence of its own, not that the body should be destroyed, but that its concupiscence, which is its evil habit, should be completely conquered so that it is rendered subject to the spirit as the natural order demands. Since after the resurrection the body will thrive in complete peace immortally in subjection to the spirit, in this present life we should seek that the habit of the flesh should be changed for the better lest it resist the spirit with inordinate demands. For until this is done "the flesh lusteth against the spirit: and the spirit against the flesh." The spirit does not resist in hate but in a desire for dominion, because it wishes what it loves to be subjected to something better; neither does the flesh resist in hate but because of the fetters of habit in which it is involved inveterately by the law of nature as an inheritance. Thus the spirit acts in dominating the flesh that it may destroy the evils of habit as if they constituted a perverse covenant, and it creates the peace of good custom. However, not even those who, depraved by a false opinion, detest their bodies would be prepared to lose one eye even without pain, not even if the one left could see as well as both together, unless something else which might be valued more demanded it. This and similar

[1] Gal. 5. 17.

instances sufficiently show to those who seek the truth without obstinacy how certain is the lesson of the Apostle, where he says, "No man ever hated his own flesh." And he adds, "But he nourisheth and cherisheth it, as also Christ does the Church."

XXV

26. Thus man should be instructed concerning the way of loving, that is, concerning the way of loving himself profitably. To doubt that he loves himself and desires to improve himself is madness. But he must be instructed how he should love his body so that he may care for it in an ordinate and prudent way. That he loves his body and wishes to have it safe and whole is equally obvious. But a man can love more than the health and soundness of his body. For many have been found willingly to undergo pains and loss of members so that something else which they loved more might be pursued. Yet a man need not be told that he should not love the health and safety of his body because he loves something else more. For the miser, although he loves money, still buys himself bread. And when he does this he spends money which he loves greatly and wishes to increase, but he esteems more the health of his body which is sustained by bread. It would be superfluous to dispute further about such a transparent matter, but the error of the impious often forces us to do this.

XXVI

27. Therefore, since there was no need for a precept that anyone love himself and his own body, because we love that which we are and that which is below us and pertains to us in accordance with a constant law of nature which is also effective among beasts—for beasts also love themselves and their bodies—there remained a necessity only that we receive precepts concerning that which is equal to us and that which is above us. "Thou shalt love," He said, "the Lord thy God with thy whole heart, and with thy whole soul, and with thy whole mind," and "Thou shalt love thy neighbor as thyself.

On these two commandments dependeth the whole law and the prophets." [1] "Now the end of the commandment is charity," [2] and this is twofold: a love of God and a love of our neighbor. Thus if you think of yourself as a whole embracing both a soul and a body and your neighbor also as a whole embracing both a soul and a body—for the soul and the body constitute a man—nothing which is to be loved is omitted from these two precepts. For when love of God is placed first and the character of that love is seen to be described so that all other loves must flow into it, it may seem that nothing has been said about the love of yourself. But when it is said, "Thou shalt love thy neighbor as thyself" at the same time, it is clear that love for yourself is not omitted.

XXVII

28. He lives in justice and sanctity who is an unprejudiced assessor of the intrinsic value of things. He is a man who has an ordinate love: he neither loves what should not be loved nor fails to love what should be loved; he neither loves more what should be loved less, loves equally what should be loved less or more, nor loves less or more what should be loved equally. No sinner should be loved in that he is a sinner, and every man should be loved for the sake of God, and God should be loved for His own sake. And if God is to be loved more than any man, everyone should love God more than himself. Again, another man is to be loved more than our own bodies; for all of these things are to be loved for the sake of God, and another man can enjoy God with us while our bodies cannot do this, for the body has life only through the soul by means of which we enjoy God.

XXVIII

29. All other men are to be loved equally; but since you cannot be of assistance to everyone, those especially are to be

---

[1] Matt. 22. 37, 39-40.   [2] 1 Tim. 1. 5.

cared for who are most closely bound to you by place, time, or opportunity, as if by chance. Thus suppose you had an abundance of something which it would be well to give to someone else who lacked it, but you could not give it to two. If two came to you of whom neither took precedence either in need or in any special connection with you, you could do nothing more just than to decide by lot which one should be given that which you could not give to both. Thus in the same way among men, not all of whom you can care for, you must consider as if selected by lot each one as he is able to be more closely associated with you in time.

XXIX

30. Among those who are able to enjoy God with us, we love some whom we help, some by whom we are helped, some whose help we need and whose wants we supply, and some on whom we bestow no benefits and from whom we await none ourselves. Be that as it may, we should desire that all enjoy God with us and that all the assistance we give them or get from them should be directed toward this end. If in the idle following of the theaters a man loves a certain actor and enjoys his art as a great good or even as the greatest good, he loves all those who share his love for the actor, not on their own account, but on account of him whom they love together. And the more fervent is his love for the actor, the more he will behave in every way possible so that he will be loved by many, and the more he will wish that many people can see him. If he sees anyone more indifferent, he excites him as much as he can with the praises of the actor. If he finds anyone opposed to the actor, he most vehemently hates in that man the hate of his beloved, and he strives to remove that feeling in every possible way. Does not this pattern of behavior befit the action of us who are united in the brotherhood of the love of God, to enjoy whom is to live the blessed life, and to whom all who love Him owe not only the fact that they exist at all but also the fact that they love Him? We

have no fear that anyone who knows Him could be displeased. And He wishes to be loved, not for selfish ends, but so that He may confer an eternal reward on those who love Him, which is the very object of their love. Thus it is that we also love our enemies. For we do not fear them, since they cannot take away that which we love. Rather are we sorry for them, for the more they hate us, the further removed are they from that which we love. If they were to turn to Him and love Him as the source of blessedness, they would necessarily love us also as companions in a great good.

XXX

31. At this point some considerations arise concerning the angels. They are blessed in the enjoyment of that which we desire to enjoy. And to the extent that we in this life enjoy Him "through a glass" or "in a dark manner" [1] we shall sustain our pilgrimage with more tolerance and more ardently desire to end it. But it may be asked reasonably whether the two precepts of love apply to the angels. For that no man was excepted when He commanded that we should love our neighbor, both Our Lord in the gospel and St. Paul the Apostle testify. And when he to whom the precepts were shown and to whom it was said that all the law and the prophets depend on them asked, "And who is my neighbor?", the Lord told of a certain man who went down from Jerusalem into Jericho and fell among thieves, and having been gravely wounded by them, was left injured and almost dead. And He taught that no one was a neighbor except the one who was merciful in healing and caring for the wounded man, putting it in such a way that the questioner himself acknowledged the truth when he was asked. Then Our Lord said to him, "Go, and do thou in like manner." [2] Thus we should understand that he is our neighbor to whom the office of mercy should be shown if he needs it, or would be shown it in the event that he did need it. It follows that he also is our neighbor who in turn shows this

[1] 1 Cor. 13. 12.   [2] Luke 10. 29-37.

office to us. The word "neighbor" denotes an object near to something else, and no one can be a neighbor unless he can be near. Who does not see that none can be denied the office of mercy when it should be extended even to our enemies? For Our Lord also said, "Love your enemies; do good to them that hate you." [3]

32. And Paul the Apostle teaches the same thing when he says: "For thou shalt not commit adultery, thou shalt not kill, thou shalt not steal, thou shalt not bear false witness, thou shalt not covet; and if there be any other commandment, it is comprised in this word: thou shalt love thy neighbor as thyself. The love of thy neighbor worketh no evil." [4] Therefore whoever thinks that the Apostle was not enjoining all men is forced to the most absurd and most shameful conclusion that the Apostle did not think it a sin if anyone committed adultery with the wife of one who was not a Christian or an enemy, or killed him or coveted his goods. If it is madness to say this, it is manifest that every man is to be thought of as a neighbor, for evil must be committed toward no one.

33. Thus if he is most justly called a neighbor to whom the office of mercy is to be shown or from whom it is to be expected, it is clear that this command in accordance with which we are enjoined to love our neighbor also includes the holy angels by whom so many works of mercy are performed for us, as we may easily see in many places of the divine Scriptures. On the basis of this principle, Our Lord God Himself wished to be called our neighbor. For Our Lord Jesus Christ signified himself to be the helper of the man lying dead in the road afflicted and abandoned by thieves. And the prophet says in his prayer, "As a neighbor and as an own brother, so did I please." [5] But since the divine substance is more excellent than ours and above us, the precept in accordance with which we are to love God is separate from that enjoining love for our neighbor. For He shows us mercy in accordance with His own goodness, while we show mercy for the sake of His goodness

[3] Matt. 5. 44.   [5] Ps. 34. 14 [35. 14].
[4] Rom. 13. 9-10.

rather than for our own; that is, He has mercy on us that we may enjoy Him, and we have mercy on our neighbor so that we may enjoy Him.

XXXI

34. On account of this principle it may still seem ambiguous when we say that we have full enjoyment of that thing which we love for its own sake, and that we should enjoy anything only in so far as it makes us blessed, merely using everything else. For God loves us, and the Divine Scripture comments on His great love for us. How does He love us? So that He may use us, or so that He may enjoy us? If He enjoys us, He needs some good of ours, but no sane person would say this. For every good of ours either is God or comes from God. To whom is it obscure or doubtful that a light does not need the brightness of the thing it illuminates? For the prophet says most openly, "I have said to the Lord, thou art my God, for thou hast no need of my goods." [1] Therefore He does not enjoy us but uses us. For if He did neither, I cannot see how He could love us.

XXXII

35. But He does not use a thing as we do. For we refer the things that we use to the enjoyment of the goodness of God; but God refers His use of us to His own good. Because He is good, we are; and in so far as we are, we are good. Moreover, since He is just, we are not wicked without punishment; and in so far as we are evil, to that extent is our being lessened. For He is the highest and first being who is altogether immutable and who could say with fullest significance, "I am who am," and "Say to them, 'He who is, hath sent me to you.'" [2] In this way other things which are cannot be unless they take their existence from Him, and they are good only in so far as He grants them existence. That use which God is said to make of us is made not to His utility but to ours, and in so far as He

[1] Ps. 15. 2 [16. 2].   [2] Cf. Exod. 3. 14.

is concerned refers only to His goodness. When we are merciful to anyone and assist him, we do so for his utility, which is our goal; but in a curious way our own utility follows as a consequence when God does not leave that compassion which we expend on one who needs it without reward. The greatest reward is that we enjoy Him and that all of us who enjoy Him may enjoy one another in Him.

XXXIII

36. For if we find complete enjoyment in ourselves we remain on the road and place our hopes of blessedness in a man or in an angel. Thus the proud man or the proud angel places his enjoyment in himself and rejoices that others place their hopes in him also. But the holy man and the holy angel refresh us with what they have received, and only with what they have received, either for themselves or for us, and even though we are wearied and desire to rest and to remain with them, they urge us onward when we have been refreshed toward Him in whose enjoyment we may both be blessed. For even the Apostle exclaims: "Was Paul then crucified for you? Or were you baptized in the name of Paul? " [1] And he says also: " Neither he that planteth is anything, nor he that watereth; but God that giveth the increase." [2] And the angel admonishes the man adoring him that he should rather adore Him under whose lordship he also serves.[3]

37. When you enjoy a man in God, it is God rather than the man whom you enjoy; for you take joy in Him who will make you blessed, and you will rejoice that you have reached Him in whom you place your hope that you may come. Whence Paul wrote to Philemon, "Yea, brother," he said, "may I enjoy thee in the Lord." [4] If he had not added "in the Lord" but had said merely "I enjoy thee," he would have placed his hope of blessedness in Philemon. However, enjoyment is very like use with delight. When that which is loved is near, it

---

[1] 1 Cor. 1. 13.   [3] Cf. Apoc. 19. 10.
[2] 1 Cor. 3. 7.   [4] Philemon 20.

necessarily brings delight with it also. If you pass on through
this delight and have referred it to that goal where you should
remain, you are using it and may only improperly be said to
enjoy it. But if you cling to that delight and remain in it, making it the end of your rejoicing, then you may truly and properly be said to be enjoying it. And this kind of enjoyment
should not be indulged except with reference to the Trinity,
which is the highest good and is immutable.

XXXIV

38. Consider that although Truth itself, and that Word
through whom all things were made, was made flesh that it
might dwell among us; [1] the Apostle yet says, "And if we have
known Christ according to the flesh, but now we know him so
no longer." [2] He wished to assume flesh not only for those ar-
riving at their estate but also to prepare the way for those setting
out at the beginning of their journey, whence it is also said,
"The Lord created me from the beginning of his ways," [3] so
that those who wished to come might have a beginning in
Him. Thus the Apostle, although he was still walking on the
road and following God who was calling him to the glory of
his Heavenly vocation, yet "forgetting the things that are be-
hind and stretching forth to those that are before," [4] he had
already passed the beginning of the ways. That is, he was no
longer in need of that which is an approach and a setting out
on the journey to all those who wish to arrive at truth and to
rest in eternal life. Thus He says, "I am the way, and the
truth, and the life"; that is, you are to come through me, to
arrive at me, and to remain in me. When we arrive at Him,
we arrive also at the Father [5]—since by an equal another equal
is known—binding and, as it were, cementing ourselves in the
Holy Spirit through whom we may remain in the highest
good, which is also immutable. Thus it may be understood

1 Cf. John 1. 3, 14.   4 Cf. Phil. 3. 13.
2 2 Cor. 5. 16.   5 Cf. John 14. 6, 10.
3 Cf. Prov. 8. 22.

that nothing should hold us on the road, for the Lord Himself, although He saw fit to become our road, did not wish to hold us upon it, but wished that we pass on, lest we cling in infirmity to temporal things, even though He took them up and wore them for our salvation. Rather let us run through them quickly that we may be worthy to approach and to reach Him who freed our nature from temporal things and made a place for it on the right hand of the Father.

XXXV

39. The sum of all we have said since we began to speak of things thus comes to this: it is to be understood that the plenitude and the end of the Law and of all the sacred Scriptures is the love of a Being which is to be enjoyed and of a being that can share that enjoyment with us, since there is no need for a precept that anyone should love himself. That we might know this and have the means to implement it, the whole temporal dispensation was made by divine Providence for our salvation. We should use it, not with an abiding but with a transitory love and delight like that in a road or in vehicles or in other instruments, or, if it may be expressed more accurately, so that we love those things by which we are carried along for the sake of that toward which we are carried.

XXXVI

40. Whoever, therefore, thinks that he understands the divine Scriptures or any part of them so that it does not build the double love of God and of our neighbor does not understand it at all. Whoever finds a lesson there useful to the building of charity, even though he has not said what the author may be shown to have intended in that place, has not been deceived, nor is he lying in any way. Lying involves the will to speak falsely; thus we find many who wish to lie, but no one who wishes to be deceived. Since a man lies knowingly but suffers deception unwittingly, it is obvious that in a given instance a man who is deceived is better than a man who lies, be-

cause it is better to suffer iniquity than to perform it. Everyone who lies commits iniquity, and if anyone thinks a lie may sometimes be useful, he must think that iniquity is sometimes useful also. But no one who lies keeps faith concerning that about which he lies. For he wishes that the person to whom he lies should have that faith in him which he does not himself keep when he lies. But every violator of faith is iniquitous. Either iniquity is sometimes useful, which is impossible, or a lie is always useless.

41. But anyone who understands in the Scriptures something other than that intended by them is deceived, although they do not lie. However, as I began to explain, if he is deceived in an interpretation which builds up charity, which is the end of the commandments, he is deceived in the same way as a man who leaves a road by mistake but passes through a field to the same place toward which the road itself leads. But he is to be corrected and shown that it is more useful not to leave the road, lest the habit of deviating force him to take a crossroad or a perverse way.

XXXVII

In asserting rashly that which the author before him did not intend, he may find many other passages which he cannot reconcile with his interpretation. If he acknowledges these to be true and certain, his first interpretation cannot be true, and under these conditions it happens, I know not why, that, loving his own interpretation, he begins to become angrier with the Scriptures than he is with himself. And if he thirsts persistently for the error, he will be overcome by it. "For we walk by faith and not by sight," [1] and faith will stagger if the authority of the Divine Scriptures wavers. Indeed, if faith staggers, charity itself languishes. And if anyone should fall from faith, it follows that he falls also from charity, for a man cannot love that which he does not believe to exist. On the other hand, a man who both believes and loves, by doing well and by obey-

[1] 2 Cor. 5. 7.

ing the rules of good customs, may bring it about that he may hope to arrive at that which he loves. Thus there are these three things for which all knowledge and prophecy struggle: faith, hope, and charity.

XXXVIII

42. But the vision we shall see will replace faith, and that blessedness to which we are to come will replace hope; and when these things are falling away, charity will be increased even more. If we love in faith what we have not seen, how much more will we love it when we begin to see it? And if we love in hope what we have not attained, how much more will we love it when we have attained it? Between temporal and eternal things there is this difference: a temporal thing is loved more before we have it, and it begins to grow worthless when we gain it, for it does not satisfy the soul, whose true and certain rest is eternity; but the eternal is more ardently loved when it is acquired than when it is merely desired. It is possible for no one desiring it to expect it to be more valuable than it actually is so that he may find it less worthy than he expected it to be. However highly anyone approaching it may value it, he will find it more valuable when he attains it.

XXXIX

43. Thus a man supported by faith, hope, and charity, with an unshaken hold upon them, does not need the Scriptures except for the instruction of others. And many live by these three things in solitude without books. Whence in these persons I think the saying is already exemplified, "whether prophecies shall be made void, or tongues shall cease, or knowledge shall be destroyed." [1] In them, as if by instruments of faith, hope, and charity, such an erudition has been erected that, holding fast to that which is perfect, they do not seek that which is only partially so [2]—perfect, that is, in so far as perfection is possible in this life. For in comparison with the life

---

[1] 1 Cor. 13. 8.   [2] 1 Cor. 13. 10.

to come, the life of no just and holy man is perfect here. Hence "there remain," he says, "faith, hope, and charity, these three: but the greatest of these is charity." [3] And when anyone shall reach the eternal, two of these having fallen away, charity will remain more certain and more vigorous.

XL

44. Therefore, when anyone knows the end of the commandments to be charity "from a pure heart, and a good conscience, and an unfeigned faith," [1] and has related all of his understanding of the Divine Scriptures to these three, he may approach the treatment of these books with security. For when he says "charity" he adds "from a pure heart," so that nothing else would be loved except that which should be loved. And he joins with this "a good conscience" for the sake of hope, for he in whom there is the smallest taint of bad conscience despairs of attaining that which he believes in and loves. Third, he says "an unfeigned faith." If our faith involves no lie, then we do not love that which is not to be loved, and living justly, we hope for that which will in no way deceive our hope.

With this I have said as much as I wished to say concerning faith at the present time, since in other books either by others or by myself much has already been said. Then may this be the limit to this book. In the remainder we shall discuss signs, in so far as God has granted us ability.

[3] 1 Cor. 13. 13.   [1] 1 Tim. 1. 5.

BOOK TWO

I

1. Just as I began, when I was writing about things, by warning that no one should consider them except as they are, without reference to what they signify beyond themselves, now when I am discussing signs I wish it understood that no one should consider them for what they are but rather for their value as signs which signify something else. A sign is a thing which causes us to think of something beyond the impression the thing itself makes upon the senses. Thus if we see a track, we think of the animal that made the track; if we see smoke, we know that there is a fire which causes it; if we hear the voice of a living being, we attend to the emotion it expresses; and when a trumpet sounds, a soldier should know whether it is necessary to advance or to retreat, or whether the battle demands some other response.

2. Among signs, some are natural and others are conventional. Those are natural which, without any desire or intention of signifying, make us aware of something beyond themselves, like smoke which signifies fire. It does this without any will to signify, for even when smoke appears alone, observation and memory of experience with things bring a recognition of an underlying fire. The track of a passing animal belongs to this class, and the face of one who is wrathful or sad signifies his emotion even when he does not wish to show that he is wrathful or sad, just as other emotions are signified by the expression even when we do not deliberately set out to show them. But it is not proposed here to discuss signs of this type. Since the class formed a division of my subject, I could not disregard it completely, and this notice of it will suffice.

II

3. Conventional signs are those which living creatures show to one another for the purpose of conveying, in so far as they

are able, the motion of their spirits or something which they have sensed or understood. Nor is there any other reason for signifying, or for giving signs, except for bringing forth and transferring to another mind the action of the mind in the person who makes the sign. We propose to consider and to discuss this class of signs in so far as men are concerned with it, for even signs given by God and contained in the Holy Scriptures are of this type also, since they were presented to us by the men who wrote them. Animals also have signs which they use among themselves, by means of which they indicate their appetites. For a cock who finds food makes a sign with his voice to the hen so that she runs to him. And the dove calls his mate with a cry or is called by her in turn, and there are many similar examples which may be adduced. Whether these signs, or the expression or cry of a man in pain, express the motion of the spirit without intention of signifying or are truly shown as signs is not in question here and does not pertain to our discussion, and we remove this division of the subject from this work as superfluous.

III

4. Among the signs by means of which men express their meanings to one another, some pertain to the sense of sight, more to the sense of hearing, and very few to the other senses. For when we nod, we give a sign only to the sight of the person whom we wish by that sign to make a participant in our will. Some signify many things through the motions of their hands, and actors give signs to those who understand with the motions of all their members as if narrating things to their eyes. And banners and military standards visibly indicate the will of the captains. And all of these things are like so many visible words. More signs, as I have said, pertain to the ears, and most of these consist of words. But the trumpet, the flute, and the harp make sounds which are not only pleasing but also significant, although as compared with the number of verbal signs the number of signs of this kind are few. For words have

come to be predominant among men for signifying whatever
the mind conceives if they wish to communicate it to anyone.
However, Our Lord gave a sign with the odor of the ointment
with which His feet were anointed; [1] and the taste of the
sacrament of His body and blood signified what He wished; [2]
and when the woman was healed by touching the hem of His
garment,[3] something was signified. Nevertheless, a multitude of
innumerable signs by means of which men express their
thoughts is made up of words. And I could express the meaning of all signs of the type here touched upon in words, but I
would not be able at all to make the meanings of words clear
by these signs.

IV

5. But because vibrations in the air soon pass away and remain no longer than they sound, signs of words have been
constructed by means of letters. Thus words are shown to the
eyes, not in themselves but through certain signs which stand
for them. These signs could not be common to all peoples
because of the sin of human dissension which arises when
one people seizes the leadership for itself. A sign of this pride
is that tower erected in the heavens where impious men deserved that not only their minds but also their voices should be
dissonant.[1]

Tower of Babel

V

6. Thus it happened that even the Sacred Scripture, by which
so many maladies of the human will are cured, was set forth in
one language, but so that it could be spread conveniently
through all the world it was scattered far and wide in the various languages of translators that it might be known for the
salvation of peoples who desired to find in it nothing more than

---

1 John 12. 3-8. For the "odor of the ointment," see 3. 12. 18.
2 Matt. 26. 28; Luke 22. 19-20.
3 Matt. 9. 20-22.   1 Cf. Gen. 11. 1-9.

the thoughts and desires of those who wrote it and through these the will of God, according to which we believe those writers spoke.

VI

7. But many and varied obscurities and ambiguities deceive those who read casually, understanding one thing instead of another; indeed, in certain places they do not find anything to interpret erroneously, so obscurely are certain sayings covered with a most dense mist. I do not doubt that this situation was provided by God to conquer pride by work and to combat disdain in our minds, to which those things which are easily discovered seem frequently to become worthless. For example, it may be said that there are holy and perfect men with whose lives and customs as an exemplar the Church of Christ is able to destroy all sorts of superstitions in those who come to it and to incorporate them into itself, men of good faith, true servants of God, who, putting aside the burden of the world, come to the holy laver of baptism and, ascending thence, conceive through the Holy Spirit and produce the fruit of a twofold love of God and their neighbor. But why is it, I ask, that if anyone says this he delights his hearers less than if he had said the same thing in expounding that place in the Canticle of Canticles where it is said of the Church, as she is being praised as a beautiful woman, "Thy teeth are as flocks of sheep, that are shorn, which come up from the washing, all with twins, and there is none barren among them" ? [1] Does one learn anything else besides that which he learns when he hears the same thought expressed in plain words without this similitude? Nevertheless, in a strange way, I contemplate the saints more pleasantly when I envisage them as the teeth of the Church cutting off men from their errors and transferring them to her body after their hardness has been softened as if by being bitten and chewed. I recognize them

[1] Cant. [Song of Sol.] 4. 2.

most pleasantly as shorn sheep having put aside the burdens of the world like so much fleece, and as ascending from the washing, which is baptism, all to create twins, which are the two precepts of love, and I see no one of them sterile of this holy fruit.

8. But why it seems sweeter to me than if no such similitude were offered in the divine books, since the thing perceived is the same, is difficult to say and is a problem for another discussion. For the present, however, no one doubts that things are perceived more readily through similitudes and that what is sought with difficulty is discovered with more pleasure. Those who do not find what they seek directly stated labor in hunger; those who do not seek because they have what they wish at once frequently become indolent in disdain. In either of these situations indifference is an evil. Thus the Holy Spirit has magnificently and wholesomely modulated the Holy Scriptures so that the more open places present themselves to hunger and the more obscure places may deter a disdainful attitude. Hardly anything may be found in these obscure places which is not found plainly said elsewhere.

VII

9. Before all it is necessary that we be turned by the fear of God toward a recognition of His will,[1] so that we may know what He commands that we desire and what He commands that we avoid. Of necessity this fear will lead us to thought of our mortality and of our future death and will affix all our proud motions, as if they were fleshly members fastened with nails, to the wood of the cross. Then it is necessary that we become meek through piety so that we do not contradict Divine Scripture, either when it is understood and is seen to attack some of our vices, or when it is not understood and we feel as though we are wiser than it is and better able to give precepts. But we should rather think and believe that which

[1] Cf. Ps. 110. 10 [111. 10]; Prov. 1. 7; 9. 10; Ecclus. 1. 16.

is written to be better and more true than anything which we could think of by ourselves, even when it is obscure.

10. After these two steps of fear and piety the third step of knowledge confronts us, which I now propose to treat. In this every student of the Divine Scriptures must exercise himself, having found nothing else in them except, first, that God is to be loved for Himself, and his neighbor for the sake of God; second, that he is to love God with all his heart, with all his soul, and with all his mind; and third, that he should love his neighbor as himself, that is, so that all love for our neighbor should, like all love for ourselves, be referred to God. Concerning these two precepts we have written in the previous book, where we discussed things. Then it follows that the student first will discover in the Scriptures that he has been enmeshed in the love of this world, or of temporal things, a love far remote from the kind of love of God and of our neighbor which Scripture itself prescribes. Then, indeed, that fear which arises from the thought of God's judgment, and that piety which can do nothing except believe in and accede to the authority of the sacred books, will force him to lament his own situation. For this knowledge of a good hope thrusts a man not into boasting but into lamentation. This attitude causes him to ask with constant prayers for the consolation of divine assistance lest he fall into despair, and he thus enters the fourth step of fortitude, in which he hungers and thirsts for justice. And by means of this affection of the spirit he will extract himself from all mortal joy in transitory things, and as he turns aside from this joy, he will turn toward the love of eternal things, specifically toward that immutable unity which is the Trinity.

11. When, in so far as he is able, he has seen this Trinity glowing in the distance, and has discovered that because of his weakness he cannot sustain the sight of that light, he purges his mind, which is rising up and protesting in the appetite for inferior things, of its contaminations, so that he comes to the fifth step, the counsel of mercy. Here he eagerly

exercises the love of his neighbor and perfects himself in it; and now, filled with hope and fortified in strength, when he arrives at the love of his enemy he ascends to the sixth step, where he cleanses that eye through which God may be seen, in so far as He can be seen by those who die to the world as much as they are able. For they are able to see only in so far as they are dead to this world; in so far as they live in it, they do not see. And now although the light of the Trinity begins to appear more certainly, and not only more tolerably but also more joyfully, it is still said to appear "through a glass in a dark manner" [2] for "we walk more by faith than by sight" [3] when we make our pilgrimage in this world, although "our community is in heaven." [4] On this step he so cleanses the eye of his heart that he neither prefers his neighbor to the Truth nor compares him with it, nor does he do this with himself because he does not so treat him whom he loves as himself. Therefore this holy one will be of such simple and clean heart that he will not turn away from the Truth either in a desire to please men or for the sake of avoiding any kind of adversities to himself which arise in this life. Such a son ascends to wisdom, which is the seventh and last step, where he enjoys peace and tranquillity. "For the fear of the Lord is the beginning of wisdom." From fear to wisdom the way extends through these steps.

VIII

12. But let us turn our attention to the third step which I have decided to treat as the Lord may direct my discourse. He will be the most expert investigator of the Holy Scriptures who has first read all of them and has some knowledge of them, at least through reading them if not through understanding them. That is, he should read those that are said to be canonical. For he may read the others more securely when he has been instructed in the truth of the faith so that they

2 1 Cor. 13. 12.   4 Phil. 3. 20.
3 2 Cor. 5. 7.

may not preoccupy a weak mind nor, deceiving it with vain lies and fantasies, prejudice it with something contrary to sane understanding. In the matter of canonical Scriptures he should follow the authority of the greater number of catholic Churches, among which are those which have deserved to have apostolic seats and to receive epistles. He will observe this rule concerning canonical Scriptures, that he will prefer those accepted by all catholic Churches to those which some do not accept; among those which are not accepted by all, he should prefer those which are accepted by the largest number of important Churches to those held by a few minor Churches of less authority. If he discovers that some are maintained by the larger number of Churches, others by the Churches of weightiest authority, although this condition is not likely, he should hold them to be of equal value.

13. The whole canon of the Scriptures on which we say that this consideration of the step of knowledge should depend is contained in the following books: the five books of Moses, that is, Genesis, Exodus, Leviticus, Numbers, and Deuteronomy; one book of Josue, one of Judges, one short book called Ruth which seems rather to pertain to the beginning of Kings; then the four books of Kings and two of Paralipomenon, not in sequence, but as if side by side and running at the same time. These are made up of history and are arranged according to the sequence of time and the order of things; there are others arranged in a different order which neither follow this order nor are connected among themselves, like Job, Tobias, Esther, Judith, two books of Machabees, and two books of Esdras. The last two seem to follow the ordered history after the end of Kings or Paralipomenon. Then there are the Prophets, among which are one book of the Psalms of David, and three books of Solomon: Proverbs, the Canticle of Canticles, and Ecclesiastes. For those two books, one of which is called Wisdom and the other Ecclesiasticus, are said to be Solomon's through a certain similitude, since it is consistently said that they were written by Jesus son of Sirach. Nevertheless, since they have merited being received as authoritative,

they are to be numbered among the prophetic books. The re-
mainder are those books called Prophets in a strict sense, con-
taining twelve single books of Prophets joined together. Since
they have never been separated, they are thought of as one.
The names of the Prophets are Osee, Joel, Amos, Abdias, Jonas,
Micheas, Nahum, Habacuc, Sophonias, Aggeus, Zacharias, and
Malachias. Then there are four books of four major Prophets:
Isaias, Jeremias, Daniel, Ezechiel. The authority of the Old
Testament ends with these forty-four books. The New
Testament contains the four evangelical books, according to
Matthew, Mark, Luke, and John; the fourteen epistles of Paul
the Apostle, to the Romans, two to the Corinthians, to the
Galatians, to the Ephesians, to the Philippians, two to the
Thessalonians, to the Colossians, two to Timothy, to Titus,
to Philemon, to the Hebrews; two Epistles of Peter, three of
John, one of Jude, and one of James; a book of the Acts of the
Apostles, and a book of the Apocalypse of John.

IX

14. In all of these books those fearing God and made meek
in piety seek the will of God. And the first rule of this undertaking and labor is, as we have said, to know these books even
if they are not understood, at least to read them or to memorize them, or to make them not altogether unfamiliar to us.
Then those things which are put openly in them either as
precepts for living or as rules for believing are to be studied
more diligently and more intelligently, for the more one learns
about these things the more capable of understanding he becomes. Among those things which are said openly in Scripture
are to be found all those teachings which involve faith, the
mores of living, and that hope and charity which we have
discussed in the previous book. Then, having become familiar
with the language of the Divine Scriptures, we should turn to
those obscure things which must be opened up and explained
so that we may take examples from those things that are
manifest to illuminate those things which are obscure, bring-

ing principles which are certain to bear on our doubts concerning those things which are uncertain. In this undertaking memory is of great value, for if it fails rules will not be of any use.

X

15. There are two reasons why things written are not understood: they are obscured either by unknown or by ambiguous signs. For signs are either literal or figurative. They are called literal when they are used to designate those things on account of which they were instituted; thus we say *bos* [ox] when we mean an animal of a herd because all men using the Latin language call it by that name just as we do. Figurative signs occur when that thing which we designate by a literal sign is used to signify something else; thus we say "ox" and by that syllable understand the animal which is ordinarily designated by that word, but again by that animal we understand an evangelist, as is signified in the Scripture, according to the interpretation of the Apostle, when it says, "Thou shalt not muzzle the ox that treadeth out the corn." [1]

XI

16. Against unknown literal signs the sovereign remedy is a knowledge of languages. And Latin-speaking men, whom we have here undertaken to instruct, need two others for a knowledge of the Divine Scriptures, Hebrew and Greek, so that they may turn back to earlier exemplars if the infinite variety of Latin translations gives rise to any doubts. Again, in these books we frequently find untranslated Hebrew words, like *amen, alleluia, racha, hosanna,* and so on, of which some, although they could be translated, have been preserved from antiquity on account of their holier authority, like *amen* and *alleluia;* others, like the other two mentioned above, are said not to be translatable into another language. For there are

[1] Deut. 25. 4. For the apostolic interpretation, see 1 Cor. 9. 9; 1 Tim. 5. 18.

some words in some languages which cannot be translated into other languages. And this is especially true of interjections which signify the motion of the spirit rather than any part of a rational concept. And these two belong to this class: *racha* is said to be an expression of indignation and *hosanna* an expression of delight. But a knowledge of these two languages is not necessary for these few things, which are easy to know and to discover, but, as we have said, it is necessary on account of the variety of translations. We can enumerate those who have translated the Scriptures from Hebrew into Greek, but those who have translated them into Latin are innumerable. In the early times of the faith when anyone found a Greek codex, and he thought that he had some facility in both languages, he attempted to translate it.

XII

17. This situation would rather help than impede understanding if readers would only avoid negligence. For an inspection of various translations frequently makes obscure passages clear. For example, one translator renders a passage in the prophet Isaias: "Despise not the family of thy seed"; but another says: "Despise not thy own flesh." [1] Either confirms the other, for one may be explained by means of the other. Thus the "flesh" may be taken literally, so that one may find himself admonished that no one should despise his own body, and the "family of the seed" may be taken figuratively so that it is understood to mean "Christians" born spiritually from the seed of the Word which produced us. But a collation of the translations makes it probable that the meaning is a literal precept that we should not despise those of our own blood, since when we compare "family of the seed" with "flesh," blood relations come especially to mind. Whence, I think, comes the statement of the Apostle, who said, "If, by any means, I may provoke to emulation them who are my flesh,

[1] Isa. 58. 7 (Ancient and Vulgate versions).

and may save some of them," [2] that is, so that, emulating those who had believed, they also might believe. He calls the Jews his "flesh" because of blood relationship. Again, a text of the prophet Isaias reads: "If you will not believe, you shall not understand," and in another translation: "If you will not believe, you shall not continue." [3] Which of these is to be followed is uncertain unless the text is read in the original language. But both of them nevertheless contain something of great value for the discerning reader. It is difficult for translators to become so disparate that they do not show a similarity in one area of meaning. Thus, although understanding lies in the sight of the Eternal, faith nourishes as children are nourished with milk in the cradles of temporal things. Now "we walk by faith and not by sight." [4] Unless we walk by faith, we shall not be able to come to that sight which does not fail but continues through a cleansed understanding uniting us with Truth. On account of this principle one said, "If you will not believe, you shall not continue," and the other said, "If you will not believe, you shall not understand."

18. Many translators are deceived by ambiguity in the original language which they do not understand, so that they transfer the meaning to something completely alien to the writer's intention. Thus some codices have "their feet are sharp to shed blood," for the word *oxús* in Greek means both "sharp" and "swift." But he sees the meaning who translates "their feet swift to shed blood"; [5] the other, drawn in another direction by an ambiguous sign, erred. And such translations are not obscure; they are false, and when this is the situation the codices are to be emended rather than interpreted. The same situation arises when some, because *móschos* in Greek means "calf," do not know that *moscheúmata* means "transplantings," and have translated it "calves." This error appears in so many texts that one hardly finds anything else written,

2 Rom. 11. 14.   5 Rom. 3. 15 (from Prov. 1. 16).
3 Isa. 7. 9 (Ancient and Vulgate versions).
4 2 Cor. 5. 7.

although the sense is very clear and is supported by the succeeding words. For the expression "bastard slips shall not take deep root" [6] makes better sense than to speak of "calves," which walk on the earth and do not take root in it. The rest of the context, moreover, supports this translation.

XIII

19. Since the meaning which many interpreters, according to their ability and judgment, seek to convey is not apparent unless we consult the language being translated, and since many translators err from the sense of the original authors unless they are very learned, we must either seek a knowledge of those languages from which Scripture is translated into Latin or we must consult the translations of those who translate word for word, not because they suffice but because by means of them we may test the truth or falsity of those who have sought to translate meanings as well as words. For often not only single words but whole locutions are translated because they cannot be expressed in Latin if one wishes to adhere to the ancient and customary idiom of the Latin language. These unidiomatic expressions do not impede the understanding, but they offend those who take more delight in things when the signs for them are governed by a certain correctness. For what is called a solecism is nothing else than an arrangement of words which does not conform to the law followed by those who have spoken before us with some authority. Whether one says "among men" by saying *inter homines* or by saying *inter hominibus* does not affect the person considering things rather than signs. In the same way, what else is a barbarism except a word pronounced with letters or sounds different from those which those who spoke Latin before us were accustomed to use? Whether *ignoscere* [to forgive] is spoken with a long or short third syllable makes little difference to a man asking God to forgive his sins, in whatever way he can pronounce the word. What then is in-

6 Wisd. 4. 3.

tegrity of expression except the preservation of the customs of others, confirmed by the authority of ancient speakers?

20. The more men are offended by these things, the weaker they are. And they are weaker in that they wish to seem learned, not in the knowledge of things, by which we are truly instructed, but in the knowledge of signs, in which it is very difficult not to be proud. For even the knowledge of things frequently raises the neck unless it is disciplined by the yoke of the Lord. It does not impede the understanding of the reader to find written: "What is the land in which these dwell upon it, whether it is good or evil, and what are the cities in which these dwell in them?" [1] I consider this to be the idiom of an alien tongue rather than the expression of a more profound meaning. There is also the expression that we cannot now take away from the chant of the people: "but upon him shall my sanctification flourish." [2] Nothing is detracted from the meaning, although the more learned hearer may wish to correct it so that *florebit* is spoken instead of *floriet,* and nothing impedes the correction but the custom of the chanters. These things may easily be disregarded if one does not wish to pay attention to that which does not detract from a sound understanding. Then there is the expression of the Apostle; "The foolishness of God is wiser than men; and the weakness of God is stronger than men." [3] If anyone wished to keep the Greek idiom and say "The foolishness of God is wiser of men, and the weakness of God is stronger of men," the labor of the vigilant reader would lead him to the true meaning, but a somewhat slower reader might either not understand it or misunderstand it. For not only is such a phrase incorrect in the Latin language, it also obscures the truth in ambiguity. Thus the foolishness of men or the weakness of men might seem wiser or stronger than God's. And even *sapientius est hominibus* [wiser than men] does not lack ambiguity, although it contains no solecism. Without the illumination of the idea

[1] Cf. Num. 13. 20.
[2] Ps. 131. 18 [132. 18], with *floriet* instead of *efflorebit* as in the Vulgate.
[3] 1 Cor. 1. 25.

being conveyed it is not clear whether *hominibus* is ablative or dative. It would be better to say *sapientius est quam homines* and *fortius est quam homines,* which express the ideas "wiser than men" and "stronger than men" without any possible ambiguity.

XIV

21. We shall speak later of ambiguous signs; now we are discussing unknown signs, of which there are two forms, in so far as they apply to words. For either an unknown word or an unknown expression may impede the reader. If these come from foreign languages we must consult one who speaks those languages, or learn them ourselves if we have leisure and ability, or make a comparison of various translations. If we do not know certain words or expressions in our own language, we become familiar with them by reading and hearing them. Nothing is better commended to the memory than those types of words and expressions which we do not know, so that when one more learned appears who may be questioned, or when a passage appears in reading where the preceding or following context makes their meaning clear, we may easily with the aid of the memory refer to them and learn them. Such is the force of habit even in learning that those who are nourished and educated in the Holy Scriptures wonder more at other expressions and think them poorer Latin than those used in the Scriptures, even though these do not appear in the writings of the Latin authors. In this matter of learning a comparison and weighing of various translations is also useful. But falsity should be rejected. For those who desire to know the Sacred Scriptures should exercise their ingenuity principally that texts not emended should give way to those emended, at least among those which come from one source of translation.

XV

22. Among these translations the *Itala* is to be preferred, for it adheres to the words and is at the same time perspica-

cious regarding meaning.[1] And in emending Latin translations, Greek translations are to be consulted, of which the
Septuagint carries most authority in so far as the Old Testament is concerned. In all the more learned churches it is now
said that this translation was so inspired by the Holy Spirit
that many men spoke as if with the mouth of one. It is said
and attested by many of not unworthy faith that, although the
translators were separated in various cells while they worked,
nothing was to be found in any version that was not found in
the same words and with the same order of words in all of the
others. Who would compare any other authority with this, or,
much less, prefer another? But even if they conferred and
arrived at a single opinion on the basis of common judgment
and consent, it is not right or proper for any man, no matter
how learned, to seek to emend the consensus of so many older
and more learned men. Therefore, even though something is
found in Hebrew versions different from what they have set
down, I think we should cede to the divine dispensation by
which they worked to the end that the books which the
Jewish nation refused to transmit to other peoples, either out
of envy or for religious reasons, might be revealed so early, by
the authority and power of King Ptolemy, to the nations
which in the future were to believe in Our Lord. It may be
that the Holy Spirit judged that they should translate in a
manner befitting the people whom they addressed and that
they should speak as if with one voice. Yet, as I have said before, a comparison with those translators who adhered most
closely to the words of the original is not without use in explaining their meaning. Latin translations of the Old Testament, as I set out to say, are to be emended on the authority
of the Greeks, and especially on the authority of those who,
although there were seventy, are said to have spoken as if with
one voice. Moreover, if the books of the New Testament are
confusing in the variety of their Latin translations, they

1 For a discussion of St. Augustine's preferences among Scriptural texts,
see Maurice Pontet, *L'exégèse de Saint Augustin prédicateur* (Paris, 1946),
pp. 220 ff.

should certainly give place to the Greek versions, especially to those which are found among more learned and diligent Churches.

XVI

23. Among figurative signs, if any impede the reader, he should study them partly with reference to a knowledge of languages and partly with reference to a knowledge of things. Thus the pool of Siloe, where the Lord commanded the man whose eyes he had anointed with clay made of spittle to wash, has some value as a similitude and undoubtedly suggests some mystery [e.g., baptism], but the name Siloe in an unknown language, if it had not been interpreted for us by the Evangelist,[1] would have concealed a very important perception. In the same way many Hebrew names which are not explained by the authors of those books undoubtedly have considerable importance in clarifying the enigmas of the Scriptures, if someone were able to interpret them. Some men, expert in that language, have rendered no small benefit to posterity by having explained all of those words taken from the Scriptures without reference to place and have translated Adam, Eve, Abraham, Moses, and names of places like Jerusalem, Sion, Jericho, Sinai, Lebanon, Jordan, or whatever other names in that language are unknown to us; and since these things have been made known, many figurative expressions in the Scriptures have become clear.

24. An ignorance of things makes figurative expressions obscure when we are ignorant of the natures of animals, or stones, or plants, or other things which are often used in the Scriptures for purposes of constructing similitudes. Thus the well-known fact that a serpent exposes its whole body in order to protect its head from those attacking it illustrates the sense of the Lord's admonition that we be wise like serpents.[2] That is, for the sake of our head, which is Christ, we should offer our bodies to persecutors lest the Christian faith be in a

---

[1] John 9. 7.   [2] Matt. 10. 16.

manner killed in us, and in an effort to save our bodies we deny God. It is also said that the serpent, having forced its way through narrow openings, sheds its skin and renews its vigor. How well this conforms to our imitation of the wisdom of the serpent when we shed the "old man," as the Apostle says, and put on the "new"; [3] and we shed it in narrow places, for the Lord directs us, "Enter ye in at the narrow gate." [4] Just as a knowledge of the nature of serpents illuminates the many similitudes which Scripture frequently makes with that animal, an ignorance of many other animals which are also used for comparisons is a great impediment to understanding. The same thing is true of stones, or of herbs or of other things that take root. For a knowledge of the carbuncle which shines in the darkness also illuminates many obscure places in books where it is used for similitudes, and an ignorance of beryl or of diamonds frequently closes the doors of understanding. In the same way it is not easy to grasp that the twig of olive which the dove brought when it returned to the ark [5] signifies perpetual peace unless we know that the soft surface of oil is not readily corrupted by an alien liquid and that the olive tree is perennially in leaf. Moreover, there are many who because of an ignorance of hyssop—being unaware of its power either to purify the lungs or, as it is said, to penetrate its roots to the rocks in spite of the fact that it is a small and humble plant—are not able at all to understand why it is said, "Thou shalt sprinkle me with hyssop, and I shall be cleansed." [6]

25. An ignorance of numbers also causes many things expressed figuratively and mystically in the Scriptures to be misunderstood. Certainly, a gifted and frank person cannot avoid wondering about the significance of the fact that Moses, Elias, and the Lord Himself all fasted for forty days.[7] The knot, as it were, of this figurative action cannot be untied without a knowledge and consideration of this number. For it contains

3 Eph. 4. 22-25; Col. 3. 9-10.   5 Gen. 8. 11.
4 Matt. 7. 13.   6 Ps. 50. 9 [51. 7].
7 Exod. 24. 18; 3 Kings [1 Kings] 19. 8; Matt. 4. 2.

four tens, to indicate the knowledge of all things involved in times. The day and the year both run their courses in a quaternion: the day in hours of morning, noon, evening, and night; the year in the months of spring, summer, autumn, and winter. But while we live in these times we should abstain and fast from temporal delight because of the eternity in which we wish to live, for in the very courses of time the doctrine in accordance with which we condemn temporal things and desire the eternal is suggested. Again, the number ten signifies a knowledge of the Creator and the creature; for the trinity is the Creator and the septenary indicates the creature by reason of his life and body. For with reference to life there are three, whence we should love God with all our hearts, with all our souls, and with all our minds; and with reference to the body there are very obviously four elements of which it is made. Thus when the number ten is suggested to us with reference to time, or, that is, when it is multiplied by four, we are admonished to live chastely and continently without temporal delight, or, that is, to fast for forty days. This the Law, represented in the person of Moses; the Prophets, whose person is acted by Elias; and the Lord Himself all admonish. He, as if bearing the testimony of the Law and the Prophets, appeared between these two on the Mount to His three watching and amazed disciples.[8] Then it may be asked how the number fifty, which is very sacred in our religion because of the feast of Pentecost, proceeds from forty; or how, when it is tripled because of the three times—before the Law, during the Law, and under Grace—or because of the name of the Father, the Son, and the Holy Spirit, and the number of the most high Trinity is added, it refers to the mystery of the most pure Church and arrives at the number of the hundred and fifty-three fish which the net caught "on the right side" after the Resurrection of the Lord.[9] In the same way many other numbers and patterns of numbers are placed by way of similitudes in the sacred books as secrets which are often closed to readers because of ignorance of numbers.

8 Matt. 17. 3.   9 John 21. 6-11.

26. An ignorance of some things concerning music also halts and impedes the reader. A certain writer has well explained some figures of things on the basis of the difference between the psaltery and the harp. It may be inquired not unreasonably among the learned whether the psalterium of ten strings follows any musical law which demands strings of that number, or, if no such law exists, whether that number should be considered more sacred either on account of the Ten Commandments (if a question is raised about that number, we can apply it to the Creator and the creature), or whether it is used because of the explanation of the number ten we have used above. And the number mentioned in the Gospel in connection with the building of the temple, forty-six years,[10] somehow has a musical sound, and, when it is applied to the structure of Our Lord's body, it causes some heretics to confess the Son of God to be clothed not falsely but with a true and human body.[11] And we find both number and music given an honorable position in many places in the Sacred Scriptures.

XVII

27. We must not listen to the superstition of the pagans who professed that the nine Muses are the daughters of Jove and Memory. They were refuted by Varro, than whom among the pagans I know of no one more eager and learned in such matters. He says that a certain city, the name of which I have forgotten, contracted with three sculptors for triple statues of the Muses to be placed as an offering in the temple of Apollo with the stipulation that only the group of the artist who wrought most beautifully would be purchased. It so happened that the work of the sculptors was of equal beauty and that the city was pleased with all nine figures so that all were bought and dedicated in the temple. He says that later the poet Hesiod named all nine of them. Thus Jupiter did not

10 John 2. 20.
11 Cf. 2. 28. 42. The number 46 was taken as a sign of Christ's human body, since A D A M may be thought of as 1 plus 4 plus 1 plus 40.

beget the nine Muses, but three artists made triple statues. Moreover, that city did not hit on the number three because someone had seen three Muses in a dream, or because so many had appeared to anyone's eyes, but because it is easy to see that all sound which furnishes material for songs is of a threefold nature. It is either produced by the voice, like the sound made by those who sing from the throat without instrumental accompaniment, by the breath, like the sound made by trumpets and flutes, or by striking, like the sound produced by harps, drums, or other percussion instruments.

XVIII

28. But whether Varro's account is to be accepted or not, we should not avoid music because of the superstition of the profane if we can find anything in it useful for understanding the Holy Scriptures, although we should not turn to their theatrical frivolities to discover whether anything valuable for spiritual purposes is to be gathered from their harps and other instruments. But we should not think that we ought not to learn literature because Mercury is said to be its inventor, nor that because the pagans dedicated temples to Justice and Virtue and adored in stones what should be performed in the heart, we should therefore avoid justice and virtue. Rather, every good and true Christian should understand that wherever he may find truth, it is his Lord's. And confessing and acknowledging this truth also in the sacred writings, he will repudiate superstitious imaginings and will deplore and guard against men who "when they knew God . . . have not glorified him as God, or given thanks; but became vain in their thoughts, and their foolish heart was darkened. For professing themselves to be wise, they became fools. And they changed the glory of the incorruptible God into the likeness of the image of a corruptible man, and of birds, and of four-footed beasts, and of creeping things." [1]

[1] Rom. 1. 21-23.

XIX

29. But in order that we may explain this whole matter, which is very important, more thoroughly, I should add that there are two kinds of doctrine which are of force in the mores of the pagans. One of these concerns things which men have themselves instituted; the other concerns those things which they have seen to be firmly established or divinely ordained. That which concerns the institutions of men is partly superstitious and partly not superstitious.

XX

30. Among superstitious things is whatever has been instituted by men concerning the making and worshiping of idols, or concerning the worshiping of any creature or any part of any creature as though it were God. Of the same type are things instituted concerning consultations and pacts involving prognostications with demons who have been placated or contracted with. These are the endeavors of the magic arts, which the poets are accustomed to mention rather than to teach. To the same class belong, although they show a more presumptuous vanity, the books of haruspicy and augury. Here also belong those amulets and remedies which medical science also condemns, whether these involve enchantments, or certain secret signs called "characters," or the hanging, tying, or in any way wearing of certain things, not for the purpose of healing the body, but because of certain significations, either occult or manifest. These are given the mild name of "physics" so that they may seem not to be involved with superstitions but to be helpful to nature. Of this type are the rings hung in the top of each ear, or the little rings of ostrich bones on the fingers, or the practice of telling a person with hiccups to hold his left thumb in his right hand.

31. To these may be added a thousand vacuous observances to follow if a limb trembles or if a stone, dog, or child comes between friends walking arm in arm. The custom of kicking a stone, as if it were a destroyer of friendship, is less obnoxious

than that of hitting an innocent child with the fist if he runs
between two people walking together. And it is fitting that
sometimes children are avenged by dogs; for some persons are
so superstitious that they even dare to hit a dog that has come
between them, and not without paying for it. For sometimes
the dog quickly sends him who strikes him from a vain remedy
to a true physician. Other similar practices are the following:
to step on the threshold when you leave your house by the
front door, to go back to bed if anyone sneezes while you are
putting on your shoes, to return to the house if you stumble
going out, or, when your clothes are torn by mice, to dread
more the omen of a future evil than the actual damage.
Whence that elegant saying of Cato, who, when consulted by a
man whose shoes had been gnawed by mice, observed that
there was nothing strange about the fact, but that it would
have been strange indeed if the shoes had gnawed the mice.

XXI

32. Nor are those to be excluded from this sort of pernicious
superstition who are called *genethliaci* because they are concerned with birthdays, or, commonly, *mathematici* [judicial
astrologers]. Although these men may seek out and even find
the exact position of the stars at the time someone is born, yet
when they seek to predict on that basis either our actions or
the outcome of our actions they err greatly and sell unlearned
men into a miserable servitude. For a man who is free when
he goes to such an astrologer gives his money that he may leave
him as the servant either of Mars or of Venus, or rather of all
the stars to which those who first erred in this way and passed
their error on to posterity gave names of beasts because of
resemblances, or names of men in an effort to honor those
men. That they did so was not strange, for even in more
modern and recent times the Romans wished to give to the
star we call Lucifer the honor and the name of Caesar. Perhaps
they might have succeeded and established a tradition if his
ancestor Venus had not already occupied the estate of that

name; nor could she according to any law pass on to her descendants what she had never possessed nor sought to possess in life. But where a place was vacant and not held in honor of someone who had died earlier, the usual practice in such matters was adhered to. Thus we call the quintile and sextile months July and August, so named in honor of Julius Caesar and Augustus Caesar, and anyone who wishes may understand that in the same way the stars once moved in the sky without the names we now give them. When certain men died whose memory was honored either because of the power of kings or the pleasure of human vanity, their names were given to the stars and they themselves were thought to be thus raised to the heavens after death. But whatever they may be called by men, the stars are those which God created and arranged as He wished, and their motion, in accordance with which times vary and are distinguished, is certain.[1] It is easy to notice this motion, however it may be, at the time a person is born according to the rules discovered and written down by those whom Scripture condemns, saying; "For if they were able to know so much as to make a judgment of the world, how did they not more easily find out the Lord thereof?" [2]

XXII

33. To desire to predict at birth, on the basis of such observations, the habits, actions, and fortunes of men is a great error and a great madness. Among those who know something about this vain knowledge, the superstition may be altogether refuted. For they observe the configurations of the stars which they call constellations at the time of birth of the one concerning whom these wretched men are consulted by those even more wretched. But it may happen that twins emerge from the uterus in such rapid succession that no one can observe the interval of time between them and note it in the numbers of the constellations. Whence it follows that some twins have the same constellation. But they do not have the same fortunes

[1] Cf. Gen. 1. 14.   [2] Wisd. 13. 9.

with respect to what they do or what they suffer. Instead, they are frequently different, so that while one lives very happily, the other lives very unhappily. Thus we know that Esau and Jacob were born twins in such a way that Jacob, who was born last, was found holding with his hand the foot of his brother who went before.[1] Certainly, the day and hour of birth for these two could not be otherwise noted except in such a way that the constellation for both should be the same. Yet what a difference there was in the manners, deeds, labors, and fortunes of these two men the Scripture, now accessible to all men, testifies.

34. Nor is it pertinent to say that the least moment and the smallest portion of time which separates the births of twins is of great importance in nature and in the very rapid course of the heavenly bodies. Even when it is conceded that it matters a great deal, it cannot be discovered by the astrologer in the constellations by which he professes to foretell destinies. Therefore he does not find any difference in constellations since he must observe the same ones whether he is consulted concerning Jacob or concerning his brother. It is of no help to him if there is a difference of time in the heavens which he rashly and negligently blames when there is no difference in the chart which he fruitlessly and solicitously examines. Thus those beliefs in certain signs of things instituted by human presumption are to be classed with those which result from certain pacts and contracts with demons.

XXIII

35. For it is brought about as if by a certain secret judgment of God that men who desire evil things are subjected to illusion and deception as a reward for their desires, being mocked and deceived by those lying angels to whom, according to the most beautiful ordering of things, the lowest part of this world is subject by the law of Divine Providence. By these illusions and deceptions it happens that many things concern-

[1] Gen. 25. 26.

ing the past and future determined by these superstitious and pernicious methods of divination actually happen as they are so determined; many things happen for the diviners in accordance with their divinations, so that, enmeshed in them, they are made more curious and entangle themselves more and more in the multiple snares of a most pernicious error. This kind of fornication of the spirit is happily not passed over in silence by the Holy Scripture, nor has it frightened the soul away in such a way that it avoids these things because falsehoods are spoken by those who profess them; but rather, "if they speak to you," it says, "and it comes to pass, do not believe them." [1] If the image of the dead Samuel predicted truths to King Saul,[2] those sacrileges by which that image was called up are no less to be condemned. Again, in the Acts of the Apostles, although the woman with the Pythonical spirit gave true testimony of the apostles of the Lord, the Apostle Paul nevertheless did not spare that spirit but cleansed the woman by denouncing and driving out the demon.[3]

36. Therefore all arts pertaining to this kind of trifling or noxious superstition constituted on the basis of a pestiferous association of men and demons as if through a pact of faithless and deceitful friendship should be completely repudiated and avoided by the Christian, "not that the idol is anything," as the Apostle says, but because "the things which the heathens sacrifice, they sacrifice to devils, and not to God. And I would not that you should be made partakers with devils." [4] For what the Apostle says concerning idols and the sacrifices that are made in their honor should be understood concerning all imaginary signs which lead to the cult of idols or to the worship of a creature or its parts as God, or pertain to the concern for remedies and other observations which are not as it were publicly and divinely constituted for the love of God and of our neighbor but rather debauch the hearts of the wretched through their love for temporal things. With reference to all teachings of this kind, therefore, the society of demons is to

[1] Cf. Deut. 13. 1-3.   [3] Acts 16. 16-18.
[2] 1 Kings [1 Sam.] 28. 15-19.   [4] 1 Cor. 10. 19-20.

be feared and avoided, since they seek to do nothing under their leader the Devil but to block and cut off our return homeward. Just as human and deceptive conjectures have been established by men concerning the stars which God created and ordered, many similar speculations have been made concerning things that are born or things having their being through the administration of Divine Providence and have been set down as if according to rule to account for unusual occurrences like the foaling of a mule or the striking of lightning.

XXIV

37. All such omens are valid only in so far as through previously established imaginings, as if these were a common language, they are agreed upon with demons. Moreover, they all imply a pestiferous curiosity, an excruciating solicitude, and a mortal slavery. They were not noticed because of any innate validity, but they were made to have a validity through being noticed and pointed out. And thus they seem different to different people in accordance with their thoughts and presumptions. Those spirits who wish to deceive procure for each one those effects as they discern them by means of which he may be ensnared by his own suspicions and customary habits of thought. To use an analogy, one figure of a letter X set down in the form of a cross mark means one thing among the Latins, another among the Greeks, not because of its nature, but because of agreement and consent to its significance. And thus he who knows both languages does not use that sign with the same signification when he wishes to convey something in writing to a Greek that he implies when he writes to a man who speaks Latin. And the single sign *beta* means a letter among the Greeks but a vegetable among the Latins. When I say *lege,* a Greek understands one thing by these two syllables, a Latin understands another. Therefore just as all of these significations move men's minds in accordance with the consent of their societies, and because this consent varies, they move them differently, nor do men agree upon them because

of an innate value, but they have a value because they are agreed upon, in the same way those signs which form the basis for a pernicious alliance with demons are of value only in accordance with the observations of the individual. This fact is very obvious in the rites of the augurs who arrange not to see birds nor to hear their cries before or after their observations because what they see or hear is significant only if the observer consents to consider it so.

XXV

38. When these things have been cut off and eradicated from the Christian mind, then those practices are to be examined which are not superstitious, that is, which are not based upon agreements with demons but upon agreements among men themselves. For all practices which have value among men because men agree among themselves that they are valuable are human institutions; and of these some are superfluous and extravagant, others useful and necessary. Thus if those signs which the actors make in their dances had a natural meaning and not a meaning dependent on the institution and consent of men, the public crier in early times would not have had to explain to the Carthaginian populace what the dancer wished to convey during the pantomime. Many old men still remember the custom, as we have heard them say. And they are to be believed, for even now if anyone unacquainted with such trifles goes to the theater and no one else explains to him what these motions signify, he watches the performance in vain. It is true that everyone seeks a certain verisimilitude in making signs so that these signs, in so far as is possible, may resemble the things that they signify. But since one thing may resemble another in a great variety of ways, signs are not valid among men except by common consent.

39. Where pictures or statues are concerned, or other similar imitative works, especially when executed by skilled artists, no one errs when he sees the likeness, so that he recognizes what things are represented. And all things of this class are to be

counted among the superfluous institutions of men except
when it is important to know concerning one of them why,
where, when, and by whose authority it was made. Then there
are thousands of imagined fables and falsehoods by whose lies
men are delighted, which are human institutions. And nothing
is more typical of men among those things which they have
from themselves than what is deceitful and lying. But the useful and necessary institutions established by men with men
include whatever they have agreed upon concerning differences of dress and the adornment of the person useful for dis-
tinguishing sex or rank, and innumerable kinds of signs without which human society could not or could not easily function, including weights and measures, differences of value and
impression in coinage appropriate to specific states and
peoples, and other things of this kind. If these had not been
purely human institutions they would not vary among different peoples nor in single nations according to the will of their
leaders.

40. But all this part of human institutions helpful to the
necessary conduct of life is not to be shunned by the Christian;
rather, as such institutions are needed, they are to be given
sufficient notice and remembered.

XXVI

Human institutions are imperfect reflections of natural institutions or are similar to them. Those which pertain to association with demons, as we have said, should be completely
repudiated and disdained; those which men have established
among themselves are to be adopted in so far as they are not
extravagant and superfluous, and especially the forms of letters
without which we cannot read, and a sufficient variety of
languages, which we have discussed above. Of the same class
are the characters of the type used by those who are now called
shorthand writers. These are useful; they neither are learned
in an illicit way, nor do they enmesh anyone in superstition,

nor enervate through extravagance, if they occupy us only so far that they do not interfere with more important things to which we should devote our attention.

XXVII

41. At the same time we must not consider as human institutions those things which men did not establish but which have been fruitful subjects of investigation as they appear either in the course of time or by divine institution. Of these, some pertain to the corporal senses, others to reason. Those which pertain to the corporal senses we either believe when they are explained to us, experience when they are demonstrated to us, or infer when we have experienced them.

XXVIII

42. Thus whatever evidence we have of past times in that which is called history helps us a great deal in the understanding of the sacred books, even if we learn it outside of the Church as a part of our childhood education. For we are required to know many things in accordance with the Olympiads and the names of the consuls; and an ignorance of the consulship at the time Our Lord was born and of that at the time of His Passion has caused some to err in such a way that they thought the Lord suffered His Passion at the age of forty-six, since the Jews said that so many years were required for the building of the temple, which is a figure for the body of Our Lord.[1] Now we know that He was baptized, on the authority of the Gospel,[2] at about the age of thirty, and it is possible to estimate on the basis of His actions as they are described in this text how much longer He lived. Nevertheless, lest any shadow of doubt should arise from any other source, it can be determined more clearly and certainly on the basis of a com-

[1] Cf. John 2. 20-21.   [2] Luke 3. 23.

parison of pagan history with that of the gospel. Then it will be seen that it was not vainly said that the temple was built in forty-six years, for since the number could not refer to the age of Our Lord, it may refer to a more secret instruction concerning the human body, which the only Son of God, through whom all things are made, did not disdain to put on for our benefit.

43. With reference to the usefulness of history, if I may omit the Greeks, what a question our Ambrose solved after the calumnies of the readers and admirers of Plato, who dared to say that all the lessons of Our Lord Jesus Christ, which they were forced to admire and to teach, were learned from the writings of Plato, since it cannot be denied that Plato lived long before the advent of the Lord! Did not the famous bishop, when he had considered the history of the pagans and found that Plato had traveled in Egypt during the time of Jeremias, show that Plato had probably been introduced to our literature by Jeremias so that he was able to teach or to write doctrines that are justly commended? Pythagoras himself did not live before the literature of the Hebrew nation, in which the cult of one God took its origin and from which Our Lord came "according to the flesh," [3] was written. And from the disciples of Pythagoras these men claim that Plato learned theology. Thus from a consideration of times it becomes more credible that the Platonists took from our literature whatever they said that is good and truthful than that Our Lord Jesus Christ learned from them. To believe the latter view is the utmost madness.

44. Although human institutions of the past are described in historical narration, history itself is not to be classed as a human institution; for those things which are past and cannot be revoked belong to the order of time, whose creator and administrator is God. It is one thing to describe what has been done, another to describe what should be done. History narrates what has been done faithfully and usefully; but books of

[3] Rom. 9. 5.

haruspicy and all similar books seek to show what should be done or observed with the audacity of the author, not with the faith of a guide.

XXIX

45. There is also a type of narrative resembling description which points out to the ignorant facts about the present rather than about the past. To this class belong things that have been written about the location of places, or the nature of animals, trees, plants, stones, or other objects. We have spoken of these writings above where we taught that they are valuable for the solution of enigmas in the Scriptures, not that they should be considered as signs for superstitious remedies or machinations. For we distinguish that type from the legitimate and open type to be discussed here. For it is one thing to say, "If you drink the juice of this herb, your stomach will not hurt," and quite another to say, "If you hang this herb around your neck, your stomach will not hurt." The first course is recommended as a healthful remedy; the second is to be condemned as a super-stitious sign. Even though there are no incantations, invocations, or "characters" involved, the question often remains as to whether the thing which is to be tied or in any way attached to heal the body is valid because of the force of nature, in which case it is to be used freely, or is valid because of some signifying convention, in which case the Christian should avoid it the more cautiously the more it seems to be efficacious in doing good. For where the cause for the efficacy of a thing is hidden, the intention for which it is used is to be considered in so far as it concerns the healing or tempering of bodies either in medicine or in agriculture.

46. The stars, of which Scripture mentions only a very few, are known through description rather than narration. Although the course of the moon, which is relevant to the celebration of the anniversary of the Passion of Our Lord, is known to many, there are only a few who know well the rising or setting or other movements of the rest of the stars without

error. Knowledge of this kind in itself, although it is not allied with any superstition, is of very little use in the treatment of the Divine Scriptures and even impedes it through fruitless study; and since it is associated with the most pernicious error of vain prediction it is more appropriate and virtuous to condemn it. It contains beyond a description of present circumstances an element akin to historical narration, since on the basis of the present position and motion of the stars it is possible to trace their past courses according to rule. It also includes predictions concerning the future made according to rule which are not superstitious and portentous but certain and fixed by calculation. We do not seek to learn from these any application to our deeds and fates in the manner of the ravings of the astrologers but only information that pertains to the stars themselves. For just as he who computes the phases of the moon, when he has observed its condition today, can determine its condition at a given period of years in the past or in the future, so in the same way those who are competent can make assertions about any of the other stars. I have stated my opinion about knowledge of this kind in so far as its usefulness is concerned.

XXX

47. Among other arts some are concerned with the manufacture of a product which is the result of the labor of the artificer, like a house, a bench, a dish, or something else of this kind. Others exhibit a kind of assistance to the work of God, like medicine, agriculture, and navigation. Still others have all their effect in their proper actions, like dancing, running, and wrestling. In all of these arts experience with the past makes possible inferences concerning the future, for no artificer in any of them performs operations except in so far as he bases his expectations of the future on past experience. A knowledge of these arts is to be acquired casually and superficially in the ordinary course of life unless a particular office demands a more profound knowledge, a possibility with which we are not here concerned. We do not need to know

how to perform these arts but only how to judge them in such a way that we are not ignorant of what the Scripture implies when it employs figurative locutions based on them.[1]

XXXI

48. There remain those institutions which do not pertain to the corporal senses but to the reason, where the sciences of disputation and number hold sway. The science of disputation is of great value for understanding and solving all sorts of questions that appear in sacred literature. However, in this connection the love of controversy is to be avoided, as well as a certain puerile ostentation in deceiving an adversary. There are, moreover, many false conclusions of the reasoning process called sophisms, and frequently they so imitate true conclusions that they mislead not only those who are slow but also the ingenious when they do not pay close attention. For example, a man holding a discussion with another submits the proposition: "What I am, you are not." The other, because it is true in part, or because the speaker is deceitful and he is simple, agrees. Then the first adds, "I am a man." When this too is agreed upon, he concludes, saying, "Therefore you are not a man." As I see it, the Scripture condemns this kind of captious conclusion in that place where it is said, "He that speaketh sophistically is hateful." [2] At times a discourse which is not captious, but which is more abundant than is consistent with gravity, being inflated with verbal ornament, is also called sophistical.

49. There are also valid processes of reasoning having false conclusions which follow from the error of the disputant. An error of this kind may be led to its conclusions by a good and learned man so that the disputant, being ashamed of them, relinquishes his error. For if he maintains it, he will also be forced to maintain conclusions which he himself condemns.

[1] It should be emphasized that throughout this discussion St. Augustine is concerned primarily with the education of the Christian exegete.
[2] Ecclus. 37. 23.

For example, the Apostle did not infer the truth when he said "then Christ is not risen," or when he said "then is our preaching vain, and your faith also vain." [3] He added other things altogether false, since Christ has risen and the preaching of those who announced this fact was not vain, nor was the faith of those who believed it. But these false conclusions most truly follow from the premise of those who said that "there is no resurrection of the dead." [4] When these false conclusions, which would be true if the dead did not arise, are repudiated, the resurrection of the dead follows as a consequent. Since correct inferences may be made concerning false as well as true propositions, it is easy to learn the nature of valid inference even in schools which are outside of the Church. But the truth of propositions is a matter to be discovered in the sacred books of the Church.

XXXII

50. However, the truth of valid inference was not instituted by men; rather it was observed by men and set down that they might learn or teach it. For it is perpetually instituted by God in the reasonable order of things. Thus the person who narrates the order of events in time does not compose that order himself; and he who shows the location of places or the natures of animals, plants, or minerals does not discuss things instituted by men; and he who describes the stars or their motions does not describe anything instituted by himself or by other men. In the same way, he who says, "When a consequent is false, it is necessary that the antecedent upon which it is based be false also," speaks very truly; but he does not arrange matters so that they are this way. Rather, he simply points out an existing truth. This rule is the basis for what we have quoted from the Apostle Paul. Those whose error the Apostle wished to refute had set forth the antecedent that there is no resurrection of the dead. But the consequent follows from this antecedent that there is no resurrection of the dead that "then

3 1 Cor. 15. 13, 14.   4 1 Cor. 15. 12.

Christ is not risen," but this consequent is false. For Christ arose, so that the antecedent is false that there is no resurrection of the dead. It follows that there is a resurrection of the dead. This may be put briefly as follows: "If there is no resurrection of the dead, neither was Christ resurrected. But Christ was resurrected. Therefore there is a resurrection of the dead." The principle that if the consequent is false the antecedent must also be false was not instituted by men, but discovered. And this rule applies to the validity of inferences, not to the truth of propositions.

XXXIII

51. When the argument about resurrection is presented in this way, both the rules of inference and the meaning of the conclusion are true. Valid inferences may be made from false premises in this way. Suppose someone to have conceded, "If a snail is an animal, it has a voice." When this has been conceded and it has been shown that a snail has no voice, the antecedent is invalidated since the consequent appears that a snail is not an animal. This consequent is false, but the inference from the false antecedent is correct. Thus the truth of a proposition is inherent in itself, but the truth of a consequent depends on the opinion or agreement of the disputant. Thus, as we said above, a false premise should be led to its valid inferences so that he whose error we wish to correct will abandon it when he sees that the consequences to which it leads are to be rejected. Now it is easy to understand that just as valid consequents may be derived from false antecedents, so also true antecedents may be led to false consequents. Suppose someone should say, "If he is just, he is good," and that this proposition is granted. Then let him add, "But he is not just," and let this also be accepted. He may conclude, "He is therefore not good." Although all of these things may be true, the conclusion is not valid according to rule. For the invalidation of the antecedent does not necessarily invalidate the consequent in the way that the invalidation of the consequent also invalidates the antecedent. Although it is true when we say,

"If he is an orator, he is a man," it does not follow that we may infer "He is not a man" if we add to the first antecedent the assertion, "He is not an orator."

XXXIV

52. In this way it is one thing to know the rules of valid inference, another thing to know the truth of propositions. Concerning inferences, one learns what is consequent, what is inconsequent, and what is incompatible. It is logical that "If one is an orator, he is a man"; it is illogical that "If one is a man, he is an orator"; and the parts of "If one is a man, he is a quadruped" are incompatible. In these instances, the inferences themselves are judged. Concerning the truth of propositions, however, the rules of inference are not relevant and the propositions are to be considered in themselves. But when true and certain propositions are joined by valid inferences to propositions we are not sure about, the latter, also, necessarily become certain. There are those who boast when they have learned the rules of valid inference as if they had learned the truth of propositions. And on the other hand, there are some who know many true propositions but think ill of themselves because they do not know the rules of inference. But he who knows that there is a resurrection of the dead is better than another who knows that it follows from the proposition that there is no resurrection of the dead that "then Christ is not risen."

XXXV

53. In the same way the science of definition, division, and partition, although it may be applied to falsehoods, is neither false in itself nor instituted by men; rather it was discovered in the order of things. Although poets have used it in their fables, and false philosophers in the expression of their erroneous opinions, and even heretics or false Christians have been accustomed to use it, there is nevertheless nothing false

in the fact that in definition, division, and partition anything is to be used which is pertinent to the subject and nothing is to be used which is not pertinent. This is true even though that which is defined or distributed into its various parts is not true. For falsehood itself may be defined, when we say that a signification attributed to a thing is false when the thing itself does not justify that signification, or define the false in some other way. And this definition is true even though the false may not be true. We may also divide this subject, saying that there are two kinds of falsehood, one of which involves things that are not possible, and the other of which involves things that are possible but nevertheless do not exist. For he who says that seven and three are eleven says something that cannot be at all; but he who says that it rained, let us say, on January 1, even though it did not rain on that day, describes something that might be true. Thus the definition and division of the false may be very true, but the false itself cannot be true in any way.

XXXVI

54. There are, moreover, certain precepts for a more copious discourse which make up what are called the rules of eloquence, and these are very true, even though they may be used to make falsehoods persuasive. Since they can be used in connection with true principles as well as with false, they are not themselves culpable, but the perversity of ill using them is culpable. Men did not themselves institute the fact that an expression of charity conciliates an audience, or the fact that it is easy to understand a brief and open account of events, or that the variety of a discourse keeps the auditors attentive and without fatigue. There are other similar principles which may be employed either in false or in true causes, but which are themselves true in so far as they cause things to be known or to be believed, or move men's minds either to seek or to avoid something. And these are rather discovered than instituted.

XXXVII

55. But when these precepts are learned they are to be applied more in expressing those things which are understood than in the pursuit of understanding. However, a knowledge of inference, definition, and division aids the understanding a great deal, provided that men do not make the mistake of thinking that they have learned the truth of the blessed life when they have learned them. Moreover, it frequently happens that men more easily learn the things themselves on account of which these principles are learned than the very knotty and spiny precepts of these disciplines. It is as if one should wish to give rules for walking and admonishes that the rear foot is not to be raised until the first foot is put down, and then goes on to describe in detail how the hinges of the joints and knees are to be moved. He speaks truly, nor is it possible to walk in any other way. Yet men more easily do these things when they walk than pay attention to them while they are doing them or understand them when they are described. But those who cannot walk care about the rules much less, since they cannot try them by experience. In the same way an ingenious person more easily discerns a false conclusion than he learns the rules governing it. And a stupid person who does not discern it is much less apt to understand the rules. And in all of these things the semblances of truth more frequently delight us than prove themselves helpful to us in disputing or judging. They may make men's discernment more alert, but they may also make men malign and proud so that they love to deceive with specious arguments and questions or to think themselves great because they have learned these things and therefore place themselves above good and innocent people.

XXXVIII

56. It is perfectly clear to the most stupid person that the science of numbers was not instituted by men, but rather investigated and discovered. Virgil did not wish to have the first

syllable of *Italia* short, as the ancients pronounced it, and it was made long.[1] But no one could in this fashion because of his personal desire arrange matters so that three threes are not nine, or do not geometrically produce a square figure, or are not the triple of the ternary, or are not one and a half times six, or are evenly divisible by two when odd numbers cannot be so divided. Whether they are considered in themselves or applied to the laws of figures, or of sound, or of some other motion, numbers have immutable rules not instituted by men but discovered through the sagacity of the more ingenious.

57. But whoever delights in these things in such a way that he boasts among the unlearned, and does not seek to learn the source of the truths which he has somehow perceived and to know whence those things are not only true but immutable which he has seen to be immutable, and thus, arising from corporal appearances to the human mind, when he finds this to be mutable since it is now learned and now unlearned, does not come to understand that it is placed between immutable things above it and other mutable things below it, and so does not turn all his knowledge toward the praise and love of one God from whom he knows that everything is derived—this man may seem to be learned. But he is in no way wise.

XXXIX

58. Thus it seems to me that studious and intelligent youths who fear God and seek the blessed life might be helpfully admonished that they should not pursue those studies which are taught outside of the Church of Christ as though they might lead to the blessed life. Rather they should soberly and diligently weigh them. And if they find some which are instituted by men which vary because of the diverse wills of those who founded them and because of the base notions of those in error, and especially if they imply a society with demons through certain significations made as if through pacts or agreements, these are to be repudiated and detested. They

[1] Virg. *Aen.* 1. 2, *et passim.*

should also avoid superfluous and extravagant institutions of men. But they should not neglect those human institutions helpful to social intercourse in the necessary pursuits of life. Among other teachings to be found among the pagans, aside from the history of things both past and present, teachings which concern the corporal senses, including the experience and theory of the useful mechanical arts, and the sciences of disputation and of numbers, I consider nothing to be useful. And in all of these, the maxim is to be observed, "Nothing in excess." And this is especially true with reference to those arts pertaining to the corporal senses, since they are limited by times and places.

59. Just as certain scholars have interpreted separately all the Hebrew, Syrian, Egyptian, and other foreign names and words that appear in the Holy Scriptures without interpretation, and just as Eusebius has written a history because of questions in the divine books which demand its use, so that it is not necessary for Christians to engage in much labor for a few things, in the same way I think it might be possible, if any capable person could be persuaded to undertake the task for the sake of his brethren, to collect in order and write down singly explanations of whatever unfamiliar geographical locations, animals, herbs and trees, stones, and metals are mentioned in the Scripture. The same thing could be done with numbers so that the rationale only of those numbers which are mentioned in the Holy Scripture is explained. I have discovered that some of this material, or, indeed, almost all of it, contrary to my expectation, has already been explained and written down by good and learned Christians, but either because of common negligence or envious disregard it remains hidden. Whether the same sort of thing could be done with the science of disputation I do not know, but I suspect that it would not be possible because that knowledge is interwoven throughout the text of Scripture like so many nerves. Moreover, it is of more use to the reader in solving and explaining ambiguities, which we shall discuss later, than in clarifying unknown signs, which we are discussing now.

XL

60. If those who are called philosophers, especially the Platonists, have said things which are indeed true and are well accommodated to our faith, they should not be feared; rather, what they have said should be taken from them as from unjust possessors and converted to our use.[1] Just as the Egyptians had not only idols and grave burdens which the people of Israel detested and avoided, so also they had vases and ornaments of gold and silver and clothing which the Israelites took with them secretly when they fled, as if to put them to a better use. They did not do this on their own authority but at God's commandment, while the Egyptians unwittingly supplied them with things which they themselves did not use well.[2] In the same way all the teachings of the pagans contain not only simulated and superstitious imaginings and grave burdens of unnecessary labor, which each one of us leaving the society of pagans under the leadership of Christ ought to abominate and avoid, but also liberal disciplines more suited to the uses of truth, and some most useful precepts concerning morals. Even some truths concerning the worship of one God are discovered among them. These are, as it were, their gold and silver, which they did not institute themselves but dug up from certain mines of divine Providence, which is everywhere infused, and perversely and injuriously abused in the worship of demons. When the Christian separates himself in spirit from their miserable society, he should take this treasure with him for the just use of teaching the gospel. And their clothing, which is made up of those human institutions which are accommodated to human society and necessary to the conduct of life, should be seized and held to be converted to Christian uses.

61. For what else have many of our good faithful done? May we not see with how much gold and silver and clothing bundled up the most sweet teacher and most blessed martyr

[1] For Augustine's influence on the preservation of the Platonic tradition, see R. Klibansky, *The Continuity of the Platonic Tradition during the Middle Ages* (London, 1939).
[2] Exod. 3. 22; 11. 2; 12. 35.

Cyprian fled from Egypt? Or how much Lactantius took with him? Or how much Victorinus, Optatus, Hilary carried with them, not to speak of those still living? Or how much innumerable Greeks have taken? This was done first by that most faithful servant of God, Moses, of whom it is written that he "was instructed in all the wisdom of the Egyptians." [3] The superstitious custom of the pagans would never have accommodated all of these men with disciplines which they might find useful, especially in those times when through objections to the yoke of Christ the pagans were persecuting Christians, if it had been suspected that the knowledge would prove useful in the worship of one God, through which the vain cult of idols is abolished. But they gave their gold, silver, and clothing to the people of God fleeing from Egypt not knowing that they yielded those things which they gave "unto the obedience of Christ." [4] That which was done in Exodus was undoubtedly a figure that it might typify these things. I say this without prejudice to any other equal or better understanding.

XLI

62. When the student of Holy Scripture, having been instructed in this way, begins to approach his text, he should always bear in mind the apostolic saying, "Knowledge puffs up; but charity edifies." [1] Thus he will feel that, although he has fled rich from Egypt, he cannot be saved unless he has observed the Pasch. "For Christ our pasch is sacrificed," [2] and the sacrifice of Christ emphasizes for us nothing more than that which He said as if to those whom He saw laboring under Pharaoh: "Come to me, all you that labour, and are burdened, and I will refresh you. Take up my yoke upon you, and learn of me, because I am meek, and humble of heart: and you shall find rest to your souls. For my yoke is sweet and my burden light." [3] To whom is it thus light except to those of meek and humble heart whom knowledge does not inflate but

3 Acts 7. 22.
4 2 Cor. 10. 5.
1 1 Cor. 8. 1.

2 1 Cor. 5. 7.
3 Matt. 11. 28-30.

charity edifies? Students should remember, therefore, concerning those who once celebrated the Pasch with appearances of shadows, that when they were commanded to mark the doorposts with the blood of the lamb, they were to be marked with hyssop.[4] This is a meek and humble herb, and yet nothing is stronger or more penetrating than its roots. Thus "rooted and founded in charity," we "may be able to comprehend, with all the saints, what is the breadth, and length, and height, and depth," [5] which things make up the Cross of Our Lord. Its breadth is said to be in the transverse beam upon which the hands are stretched; its length extends from the ground to the crossbar, and on it the whole body from the hands down is affixed; its height reaches from the crossbar to the top where the head is placed; and its depth is that part which is hidden beneath the earth. In the Sign of the Cross the whole action of the Christian is described: to perform good deeds in Christ, to cling to Him with perseverance, to hope for celestial things, to refrain from profaning the sacraments. Having been cleansed by this action, we shall be able "to know also the charity of Christ, which surpasseth all knowledge," through which He is equal with the Father, by whom all things are made, so that we "may be filled unto all the fullness of God." [6] There is also in hyssop a cleansing power, lest, inflated by the knowledge of wealth taken from the Egyptians, the swollen lung should breathe forth in pride: "Thou shalt sprinkle me with hyssop, and I shall be cleansed: thou shalt wash me, and I shall be made whiter than snow. To my hearing thou shalt give joy and gladness." And then the Psalmist adds as a consequence that he may show hyssop to signify a cleansing from pride, "and the bones that have been humbled shall rejoice." [7]

XLII

63. To the extent that the wealth of gold and silver and clothing which that people took with them from Egypt was less

---

[4] Exod. 12. 22.
[5] Eph. 3. 17-18.

[6] Eph. 3. 19.
[7] Ps. 50. 9-10 [51. 7-8].

than that they afterwards acquired at Jerusalem, especially during the reign of King Solomon,[1] the knowledge collected from the books of the pagans, although some of it is useful, is also little as compared with that derived from the Holy Scriptures. For whatever a man has learned elsewhere is censured there if it is harmful; if it is useful, it is found there. And although anyone may find everything which he has usefully learned elsewhere there, he will also find very abundantly things which are found nowhere else at all except as they are taught with the wonderful nobility and remarkable humility of the Holy Scriptures. Therefore, when the reader has been prepared by this instruction so that he is not impeded by unknown signs, with a meek and humble heart, subjected easily to Christ with a burden that is light, established, rooted, and built up in charity so that knowledge cannot puff him up, let him turn next to the examination and consideration of ambiguous signs in the Scriptures, concerning which I shall essay to set forth in the third book what the Lord has granted to me.

BOOK THREE

I

1. A man fearing God diligently seeks His will in the Holy Scriptures. And lest he should love controversy, he is made gentle in piety. He is prepared with a knowledge of languages lest he be impeded by unknown words and locutions. He is also prepared with an acquaintance with certain necessary things lest he be unaware of their force and nature when they are used for purposes of similitudes. He is assisted by the accuracy of texts which expert diligence in emendation has procured. Thus instructed, he may turn his attention to the investigation and solution of the ambiguities of the Scriptures. That he may not be deceived by ambiguous signs we shall

[1] 3 Kings [1 Kings] 10. 14-17.

offer some instruction. It may be, however, that he will deride those ways which we wish to point out as puerile either because of the greatness of his acumen or the brilliance of his illumination. Nevertheless, as I set out to say, he who has a mind to be instructed by us, in so far as he may be instructed by us, will know that the ambiguity of Scripture arises either from words used literally or figuratively, both of which types we have discussed in the second book.

II

2. When words used literally cause ambiguity in Scripture, we must first determine whether we have mispunctuated or misconstrued [with reference to Latin, "mispronounced"] [1] them. When investigation reveals an uncertainty as to how a locution should be pointed or construed, the rule of faith should be consulted as it is found in the more open places of the Scriptures and in the authority of the Church. We explained this sufficiently when we spoke of things in the first book. But if both meanings, or all of them, in the event that there are several, remain ambiguous after the faith has been consulted, then it is necessary to examine the context of the preceding and following parts surrounding the ambiguous place, so that we may determine which of the meanings among those which suggest themselves it would allow to be consistent.

3. Now, consider some examples. This heretical punctuation does not allow that the Word is God: "In the beginning was the Word, and the Word was with God, and God was," so that the sense of what follows is different: "This Word was in the beginning with God." But this is to be refuted according to the rule of faith which teaches us the equality of the Trinity, so that we say: "And the Word was God. The same was in the beginning with God." [2]

4. Neither aspect of the ambiguity is contrary to the faith, so that the context must be used as a guide where the Apostle

1 On "pronunciation" here translated in other terms, see H. I. Marrou, *Saint Augustin et la fin de la culture antique* (Paris, 1938), p. 21.
2 John 1. 1-2.

says: "What I shall do I know not. But I am straitened between two: having a desire to be dissolved and to be with Christ, (for this is) a thing by far the better. But to abide still in the flesh, is needful for you." [3] It is uncertain whether this should be punctuated so as to read "having a desire for two things," or so as to read "straitened between two," so that the passage continues, "having a desire to be dissolved and to be with Christ." But since there follows "for this is a thing by far the better," he clearly says that he has a desire for the better thing, as if he were urged by two things, for one of which he has a desire and for the other of which there is a necessity. That is, he has a desire to be with Christ, but a necessity to remain in the flesh. This ambiguity is decided by one word showing a logical connection, "for" [and, in English, the expression "this is"]. The translators who have omitted this particle have been inclined toward the opinion that he was not only urged by two things but that he also desired two things. Therefore the passage should be punctuated as follows: "What I shall do I know not. But I am straitened between two." This is followed by the phrase "having a desire to be dissolved and to be with Christ." And as if answering the question why he should have more of a desire for this, he says, "for this is a thing by far the better." Why is he urged by two things? Because there is a necessity that he remain, whence he adds, "But to abide still in the flesh, is needful for you" [i.e., "on your account"].

5. But when neither the principles of the faith nor the context is sufficient to explain an ambiguity, there is nothing to prevent our punctuating the passage in any of the various possible ways. For example, the following passage occurs in Corinthians: "Having therefore these promises, dearly beloved, let us cleanse ourselves from all defilement of the flesh and of the spirit, perfecting sanctification in the fear of God. Understand us. We have corrupted no man." [4] There is a question as to whether we should interpret the text to mean "let us cleanse ourselves from all defilement of the flesh and of the spirit," according to the lesson of "that she may be holy both

---

[3] Phil. 1. 22-24.   [4] 2 Cor. 7. 1-2.

in body and spirit," [5] or, on the other hand, whether we should say "let us cleanse ourselves of all defilement of the flesh," and continue "and perfecting sanctification of the spirit in the fear of God; understand us." Distinctions in interpretation of this kind may be made at the will of the reader.

III

6. The principles that I have described for the treatment of ambiguous pointing serve also for ambiguous constructions. For these also, unless the reader is weakened by too much carelessness, are to be corrected according to the rule of faith, or according to the context established by the preceding and following passages; or, if neither of these is sufficient for correction and some doubt still remains, whatever blameless interpretation the reader wishes may be used. If faith did not remove the possibility on the grounds that we do not believe that God will accuse His elect nor that Christ will condemn them, we might read as a question, "Who shall accuse against the elect of God," and add as an answer, "God that justifieth." [1] And we might ask again, "Who is he that shall condemn?" and answer, "Christ Jesus that died." [2] But since it is utter madness to believe this, the passages should be interpreted so that the first element is a question, the second a rhetorical question. The ancients distinguished a question from a rhetorical question by saying that there are many possible answers to a question, but that a rhetorical question may be answered only negatively or affirmatively. The verses should be pronounced so that after the question, "Who shall accuse against the elect of God?", that which follows is inflected as a question, "God that justifieth?", with an implied negative reply. And in the same way we ask, "Who is he that shall condemn?", and add as a rhetorical question implying once more a negative reply, "Christ Jesus that died, yea that is risen also again; who is at the right hand of God, who also maketh intercession for us?" But in that place where the

---

[5] 1 Cor. 7. 34. [1] Rom. 8. 33. [2] Rom. 8. 34.

Apostle says, "What then shall we say? That the Gentiles, who followed not after justice, have attained to justice," ³ the context does not make sense unless the first part, "What then shall we say?", is expressed as a question and the last part, "That the Gentiles, who followed not after justice, have attained to justice," is added as a reply. However, in inflecting the question of Nathanael, "Can anything of good come from Nazareth?",⁴ I do not see how we can determine whether the whole should be stated affirmatively with interrogatory inflection only in the phrase "from Nazareth" or whether the interrogatory inflection should be applied to the whole expression. Faith impedes neither of these interpretations.

7. There is sometimes an ambiguity in the doubtful sound of syllables, and this matter also pertains to pronunciation. For example, in the passage "My bone [Latin, *os*] is not hidden from thee, which thou hast made in secret," ⁵ it is not clear to the reader whether *os* should be pronounced with a short or with a long vowel. If he makes it short, the plural form is *ossa* [bones], if he makes it long, the plural form is *ora* [mouths]. But such things may be decided by looking at the passage in an earlier language. The Greek text in this instance reads not *stóma* [mouth], but *ostéon* [bone]. As in this example, the vulgar form of speech is sometimes clearer than the more correct literary form. Indeed, I should prefer to say "My bone [*ossum meum*] is not hidden from thee," rather than to express it in a less clear but more correct Latin. But sometimes the significance of a doubtful syllable is made clear by the use of a word in the same context having a related meaning, as in this passage: "Of which I foretell [i.e., warn] you as I have foretold to you, that they who do such things shall not obtain the kingdom of God." ⁶ If he had simply said "of which I foretell" [Latin, *praedico*], without adding "as I have foretold" [Latin, *sicut praedixi*], it would not have been clear without reference to earlier texts whether the middle syllable of *praedico* should be long [meaning "I foretell"] or short [meaning

---

3 Rom. 9. 30.   5 Ps. 138. 15 [139. 15].
4 John 1. 46.   6 Gal. 5. 21.

"I announce"]. But it is evident since he said "I have fore-told" [*praedixi*] and not "I have announced" [*praedicavi*] that it should be pronounced long.

IV

8. Not only ambiguities of this type but also those which do not depend on punctuation or pronunciation should be treated in the same way. Consider the passage from Thessalonians: "Therefore we were comforted, brethren, in you." [1] It is doubt-ful whether "brethren" [Latin, *fratres*] should be read as a vocative [as in the translation above] or as an accusative [so as to read "on this account we have comforted the brethren among you"]. But in Greek the two cases do not have the same form, and when the Greek text is examined, the word is found to be vocative. But if the translator had been willing to say, *Propterea, consolationem habuimus, fratres, in vobis* [instead of *consolati sumus*], the translation would have been less literal but also less doubtful as to meaning. Or, if he had added *nostri* [i.e., "our brethren"], almost no one would have doubted that *fratres* should be construed as a vocative. But an addition of this kind would be more dangerous. It has been done in that passage from Corinthians where the Apostle says, "I die daily . . . by your glory, brethren, which I have in Christ Jesus." [2] A certain translator says, "I die daily, I protest, by your glory," because a mood of adjuration is evident in the Greek text without any ambiguous sound. Only rarely and with difficulty may we find ambiguities in the literal meanings of the scriptural vocabulary which may not be solved either by examining the context which reveals the author's intention, or by comparing translations, or by consulting a text in an earlier language.

V

9. But the ambiguities of figurative words, which are now to be treated, require no little care and industry. For at the out-

---

[1] 1 Thess. 3. 7.   [2] 1 Cor. 15. 31.

set you must be very careful lest you take figurative expressions literally. What the Apostle says pertains to this problem: "For the letter killeth, but the spirit quickeneth." [1] That is, when that which is said figuratively is taken as though it were literal, it is understood carnally. Nor can anything more appropriately be called the death of the soul [2] than that condition in which the thing which distinguishes us from beasts, which is the understanding, is subjected to the flesh in the pursuit of the letter. He who follows the letter takes figurative expressions as though they were literal and does not refer the things signified to anything else. For example, if he hears of the Sabbath, he thinks only of one day out of the seven that are repeated in a continuous cycle; and if he hears of Sacrifice, his thoughts do not go beyond the customary victims of the flocks and fruits of the earth. There is a miserable servitude of the spirit in this habit of taking signs for things, so that one is not able to raise the eye of the mind above things that are corporal and created to drink in eternal light.

VI

10. But this servitude among the Jewish people was very different from that of others, since they were subjected to temporal things in such a way that the One God was served in these things. And although they took signs of spiritual things for the things themselves, not knowing what they referred to, yet they acted as a matter of course that through this servitude they were pleasing the One God of All whom they did not see. The Apostle describes this kind of divine service as being like the behavior of children under a pedagogue.[1] In this way those who stubbornly adhered to such signs as things could hardly bear it when the time for them to be revealed had come and the Lord condemned them.[2] And hence their leaders stirred up accusations that He wrought cures on the Sabbath,[3] and the people, taking these signs as

1 2 Cor. 3. 6.   2 E.g., see Matt. 12. 1-8.
2 Cf. Rom. 8. 6.   3 Cf. Luke 6. 7.
1 Gal. 3. 24.

things, did not believe him to be God or to have come from God, since He did not treat the signs in accordance with the Jewish observance.[1] But those who did believe, of whom the first Church at Jerusalem was composed, demonstrated sufficiently the usefulness of having been in this way under the tutelage of a pedagogue so that the signs which had been temporarily imposed upon worshipers referred the belief of those observing them to the worship of one God, who made Heaven and earth. In these temporal and carnal sacrifices and signs, although they did not know how to interpret them spiritually, they devoted themselves to the worship of the Eternal God and were hence near to spiritual things. Thus they were so susceptible to the Holy Spirit that they sold everything they had and placed the proceeds "before the feet of the Apostles" [2] that they might be distributed to the needy, dedicating themselves to God as a new temple whose earthly image, which is the old temple, they were serving.

11. It is not recorded that any of the churches of the Gentiles did this because those who worshiped graven images as gods were not near enough to spiritual understanding.

VII

And if at any time any of them wished to interpret the idols as signs, they referred them to the worship and veneration of creatures. Of what use is it to me, for example, if Neptune is not taken as a god but as a sign of all the sea, or, indeed, of all other waters that rise from fountains? He is thus described by one of their poets, if I remember correctly, in the following verses:

> O Father Neptune, whose aged temples resound,
> Wreathed in the noisy sea, from whose beard eternally flows
> The vast ocean, and in whose hair the rivers wander . . . .[3]

This husk shakes sounding pebbles inside its sweet shell, but it is not food for men but for swine. He who knows the Gospels

[1] Cf. John 9. 14-18.   [2] Acts 4. 35.

[3] The author of these lines. which were formerly ascribed to Claudian, is unknown.

knows what I mean.[1] What is it to me that the statue of Neptune is referred to that meaning except to show that I should worship neither? For to me, neither any statue nor the great sea itself is a god. But I admit that those who think the works of men are gods have sunk lower than those who deify the works of God. But we are taught to love and worship one God, who made all these things whose images they venerate either as gods or as signs and images of gods. If it is a carnal slavery to adhere to a usefully instituted sign instead of to the thing it was designed to signify, how much is it a worse slavery to embrace signs instituted for spiritually useless things instead of the things themselves? Even if you transfer your affections from these signs to what they signify, you still, nevertheless, do not lack a servile and carnal burden and veil.

VIII

12. On this account Christian liberty freed those it found under useful signs, discovering them to be among those who were "nigh," [2] interpreting the signs to which they were subject, and elevating them to the things which the signs represented. From them were constituted the Churches of the holy Israelites. For those it found under useless signs it not only prohibited and destroyed all servile obligation to those signs, but also destroyed the signs themselves, so that the pagans were converted from a corruption of many simulated gods, a thing frequently and accurately called "fornication" in the Scriptures, to the cult of one God. Nor were they led to a servitude under useful signs, but rather to an exercise of the mind directed toward understanding them spiritually.

IX

13. He is a slave to a sign who uses or worships a significant thing without knowing what it signifies. But he who uses

[1] Cf. Luke 15. 16. "Food for swine" is false or empty doctrine for heretics.
[2] I.e., the Jews; Eph. 2. 17.

or venerates a useful sign divinely instituted whose signifying force he understands does not venerate what he sees and what passes away but rather that to which all such things are to be referred. Such a man is spiritual and free, even during that time of servitude in which it is not yet opportune to reveal to carnal minds those signs under whose yoke they are to be tamed. The Patriarchs and the Prophets were spiritual men of this kind, as were also all those among the people of Israel through whom the Holy Spirit ministered to us the help and solace of the Scriptures. In these times, since there has been revealed to us a clear sign of our liberty in the Resurrection of the Lord, we are not heavily burdened with the use of certain signs whose meaning we understand; rather we have a few in place of many, which the teaching of the Lord and the Apostles has transmitted to us, and these are very easy to perform, very sublime in implication, and most upright in observance. Such are the sacrament of Baptism and the celebration of the Body and Blood of the Lord. When anyone instructed perceives one of these, he knows what it refers to so that he venerates it not in carnal servitude but in spiritual freedom. But just as it is a servile infirmity to follow the letter and to take signs for the things that they signify, in the same way it is an evil of wandering error to interpret signs in a useless way. However, he who does not know what a sign means, but does know that it is a sign, is not in servitude. Thus it is better to be burdened by unknown but useful signs than to interpret signs in a useless way so that one is led from the yoke of servitude only to thrust his neck into the snares of error.

X

14. To this warning that we must beware not to take figurative or transferred expressions as though they were literal, a further warning must be added lest we wish to take literal expressions as though they were figurative. Therefore a method of determining whether a locution is literal or figurative must be established. And generally this method consists in this: that

whatever appears in the divine Word that does not literally pertain to virtuous behavior or to the truth of faith you must take to be figurative. Virtuous behavior pertains to the love of God and of one's neighbor; the truth of faith pertains to a knowledge of God and of one's neighbor. For the hope of everyone lies in his own conscience in so far as he knows himself to be becoming more proficient in the love of God and of his neighbor. Concerning these things we have spoken in the first book.

15. But since humanity is inclined to estimate sins, not on the basis of the importance of the passion involved in them, but rather on the basis of their own customs, so that they consider a man to be culpable in accordance with the way men are reprimanded and condemned ordinarily in their own place and time, and, at the same time, consider them to be virtuous and praiseworthy in so far as the customs of those among whom they live would so incline them, it so happens that if Scripture commends something despised by the customs of the listeners, or condemns what those customs do not condemn, they take the Scriptural locution as figurative if they accept it as an authority. But Scripture teaches nothing but charity, nor condemns anything except cupidity, and in this way shapes the minds of men. Again, if the minds of men are subject to some erroneous opinion, they think that whatever Scripture says contrary to that opinion is figurative. But it asserts nothing except the catholic faith as it pertains to things past, future, and present. It is a history of past things, an announcement of future things, and an explanation of present things; but all these things are of value in nourishing and supporting charity and in conquering and extirpating cupidity.

16. I call "charity" the motion of the soul toward the enjoyment of God for His own sake, and the enjoyment of one's self and of one's neighbor for the sake of God; but "cupidity" is a motion of the soul toward the enjoyment of one's self, one's neighbor, or any corporal thing for the sake of something other than God. That which uncontrolled cupidity does to corrupt the soul and its body is called a "vice"; what it does in such

a way that someone else is harmed is called a "crime." [1] And
these are the two classes of all sins, but vices occur first. When
vices have emptied the soul and led it to a kind of extreme
hunger, it leaps into crimes by means of which impediments to
the vices may be removed or the vices themselves sustained. On
the other hand, what charity does to the charitable person is
called "utility"; what it does to benefit one's neighbor is called
"beneficence." And here utility occurs first, for no one may
benefit another with that which he does not have himself. The
more the reign of cupidity is destroyed, the more charity is increased.

XI

17. Therefore whatever is read in the Scriptures concerning
bitterness or anger in the words or deeds of the person of God
or of his saints is of value for the destruction of the reign of
cupidity. If it is obviously so intended it is not to be referred
to something else as though it were figurative. An example is
afforded by this passage from the Apostle: "Thou treasurest up
to thyself wrath, against the day of wrath and revelation of
the just judgment of God, Who will render to every man according to his works: To them, indeed, who according to
patience and in good work seek glory and honor and incorruption, eternal life: But to them that are contentious, and who
obey not the truth but give credit to iniquity, wrath and indignation. Tribulation and anguish upon every soul of man
that worketh evil, of the Jew first, and also of the Greek." [2]
For this is addressed to those who do not wish to triumph over
the cupidity by which they are being destroyed. However,
this is a clear description of men in whom the power of cupidity, which once dominated, is destroyed: "And they that are
Christ's, have crucified their flesh, with the vices and concupiscences." [3] Although certain figurative words are used here
like "wrath of God" and "crucified," there are not so many

---

[1] *Flagitium* is here translated "vice," and *facinus* is translated "crime."
[2] Rom. 2. 5-9.   [3] Gal. 5. 24.

that they obscure the sense or make an allegory or enigma of the kind which I call attention to as a figurative locution. But it is said to Jeremias, "Lo, I have set thee this day over kingdoms, to root up, and to pull down, and to destroy." [4] There is no doubt that this whole expression is figurative and is to be referred to that end of which we have spoken.

XII

18. Those things which seem almost shameful to the inexperienced, whether simply spoken or actually performed either by the person of God or by men whose sanctity is commended to us, are all figurative, and their secrets are to be removed as kernels from the husk as nourishment for charity. Whoever uses transitory things in a more restricted way than is customary among those with whom he lives is either superstitious or temperate. But whoever so uses them that he exceeds the measure established by the custom of the good men among his neighbors either signifies something or is vicious. In all instances of this kind it is not the use of the things but the desire of the user which is culpable. Thus no reasonable person would believe under any circumstances that the feet of the Lord were anointed with precious ointment by the woman [2] in the manner of lecherous and dissolute men whose banquets we despise. For the good odor is good fame which anyone in the works of a good life will have when he follows in the footsteps of Christ, as if anointing His feet with a most precious odor. In this way what is frequently shameful in other persons is in a divine or prophetic person the sign of some great truth. Certainly union with a prostitute is one thing when morals are corrupted and quite another thing in the prophecy of the prophet Osee.[3] If, moreover, it is shameful to strip the body of clothing at the banquets of the drunken and lascivious, it is not on this account shameful to be naked in the baths.

[4] Jer. 1. 10.   [1] Luke 7. 37-38; John 12. 3.   [2] Osee [Hosea] 1. 2.

19. Careful attention is therefore to be paid to what is proper to places, times, and persons lest we condemn the shameful too hastily. It may be that a wise man may use the most precious food without any vice of ardor or voraciousness, but a fool may glow with the most filthy flame of gluttony before the vilest food. Any healthy man would rather eat fish as the Lord did [3] than lentils after the manner of Esau the grandson of Abraham,[4] or barley in the fashion of oxen. But because they eat coarser food it does not follow that certain beasts are more continent than we are. For in all things of this kind we are to be commended or reprimanded, not because of the nature of the things which we use, but because of the motive in using them and the way in which they are desired.

20. The just men of antiquity imagined and foretold the Heavenly Kingdom in terms of an earthly kingdom. The necessity for a sufficient number of children was responsible for the blameless custom by which one man had several wives at the same time.[5] And thus it was not virtuous for one wife to have several husbands, for one woman is not more fruitful by this means, and it is rather a whorish evil to seek either wealth or children by common intercourse. With reference to customs of this kind, whatever the holy men of those days did without libidinousness, even though they did things that may not now be done in that way, is not blamed by the Scripture. And whatever is so narrated is to be taken not only historically and literally but also figuratively and prophetically, so that it is interpreted for the end of charity, either as it applies to God, to one's neighbor, or to both. Although the ancient Romans considered it shameful to wear tunics stretching to the ankles and with long sleeves, now it is shameful for a wellborn man not to wear a tunic of that type when he puts one on. In the same way we should be cautious in the use of other things to avoid libidinousness, which not only wickedly abuses the custom of those among whom we live, but often, when it

3 Luke 24. 43.   5 E.g., Gen. 16. 3.
4 Gen. 25. 34.

trangresses the limits of that custom, shows its own foulness in a shameful upheaval from its hiding place under the cover of solemn morals.

XIII

21. Whatever, therefore, is harmonious with the custom of those among whom we live, either because of necessity or because of duty, is to be referred by good and great men to utility or to beneficence. This is to be done either literally, as we ourselves must do it, or figuratively, as is permitted to the prophets.

XIV

22. When those inexperienced in the customs of others read about these deeds, they think them to be shameful, unless they are restrained by authority. Nor can they observe that their entire way of living with respect to marriage, banquets, clothing, or other necessities and customs of human life might seem shameful among other peoples and at other times. Some, as it were somnolent, who were neither in the deep sleep of folly nor able to awaken in the light of wisdom, misled by the variety of innumerable customs, thought that there was no such thing as absolute justice but that every people regarded its own way of life as just. For if justice, which ought to remain immutable, varies so much among different peoples, it is evident that justice does not exist. They have not understood, to cite only one instance, that "what you do not wish to have done to yourself, do not do to another"[1] cannot be varied on account of any diversity of peoples. When this idea is applied to the love of God, all vices perish; when it is applied to the love of one's neighbor, all crimes disappear. For no one wishes his own dwelling corrupted, so that he should not therefore wish to see God's dwelling, which he is himself, corrupted. And since no one wishes to be harmed by another, he should not harm others.

[1] Cf. Matt. 7. 12; Luke 6. 31; Tob. 4. 16.

XV

23. Thus when the tyranny of cupidity has been overthrown, charity reigns with its most just laws of love for God for the sake of God and of one's self and of one's neighbor for the sake of God. Therefore in the consideration of figurative expressions a rule such as this will serve, that what is read should be subjected to diligent scrutiny until an interpretation contributing to the reign of charity is produced. If this result appears literally in the text, the expression being considered is not figurative.

XVI

24. If a locution is admonitory, condemning either vice or crime or commending either utility or beneficence, it is not figurative. But if it seems to commend either vice or crime or to condemn either utility or beneficence, it is figurative. "Except you eat," He says, "the flesh of the Son of man, and drink his blood, you shall not have life in you." [1] He seems to commend a crime or a vice. It is therefore a figure, admonishing communion in the Passion of Our Lord, and sweetly and usefully concealing a memorial of the fact that His flesh was crucified and wounded for us. The Scripture says, "If thy enemy be hungry, give him to eat; if he thirst, give him to drink." This undoubtedly commends a beneficence, but what follows might be taken to commend a crime of malevolence: "For, doing this, thou shalt heap coals of fire upon his head." [2] Therefore do not doubt that it is said figuratively. And since it can be interpreted in two ways, one admonishing harm, another admonishing benefit, charity should call you to beneficence so that you understand the coals of fire to be the burning sighs of penitence which heal the pride of the one who sorrows that he was an enemy of the man from whom he had received assistance for his misery. Again, when the Lord says, "He that loveth his life shall lose it," [3] it is not to be thought

[1] John 6. 54. [3] John 12. 25.
[2] Rom. 12. 20; Prov. 25. 21-22.

that the useful love by which one seeks to preserve his life should be avoided; rather, "he shall lose his life" is spoken figuratively. That is, let him cut off and put away the use of it which he now has, the perverse and unnatural use of life by which he is moved toward temporal things so that he does not seek the eternal. It is written, "Give to the merciful, and uphold not the sinner." [4] The last part of this lesson seems to condemn beneficence. It says, "Uphold not the sinner." Therefore you should understand "sinner" to be used figuratively for sin, so that you should not uphold the sin of the sinner.

XVII

25. It often happens that a person who is, or thinks he is, in a higher grade of spiritual life thinks that those things which are taught for those in lower grades are figurative. For example, if he embraces the celibate life and has made himself a eunuch for the Kingdom of Heaven,[1] he thinks it necessary to take anything the sacred books admonish concerning the love and rule of a wife as figurative rather than literal. And if anyone has sought to keep his virgin unmarried,[2] he wishes to take as figurative that passage which says, "Marry thy daughter, and thou shalt do a great work." [3] Therefore this should be added to the rules necessary for understanding the Scriptures: some things are taught for everyone in general; others are directed toward particular classes of people, in order that the medicine of instruction may be applicable not only to the general state of health but also to the special infirmities of each member. For what cannot be elevated to a higher class must be cared for in its own class.

XVIII

26. Again caution must be exercised lest anyone think that those things in the Scriptures which are neither vices nor

4 Ecclus. 12. 4.   2 1 Cor. 7. 37.
1 Cf. Matt. 19. 12.   3 Ecclus. 7. 27.

crimes among the ancients because of the condition of their times, even when such things are taken literally rather than figuratively, may be transferred to our own times and put in practice. Unless he is dominated by cupidity and seeks protection for it in the very Scriptures by means of which it is to be overthrown, no one will do this. The wretched man does not realize that these things are so arranged for this purpose: that men of good hope may profitably see both that the customs which they disdain may have a good use and that the customs which they themselves embrace may be damnable, if charity moves the first and cupidity accompanies the second.

27. For if because of the times a man could then use many wives chastely, a man may nevertheless use one wife libidinously. I commend more a man who uses the fecundity of many wives for a disinterested purpose than a man enjoying the flesh of one wife for itself. In the first instance a utility congruous with the circumstances of the time is sought; in the second a cupidity implicated in temporal delights is satiated. They are on a lower step toward God to whom the Apostle "by indulgence" allowed carnal commerce with one wife because of intemperance [1] than those who, although they had several wives, sought in intercourse with them only the procreation of children in the same way that a wise man seeks only nourishment in food and drink. And in the same way had they perceived the Advent of the Lord during their lifetimes, a time not to scatter stones but to gather them,[2] they would at once have made themselves eunuchs for the Kingdom of Heaven; for there is no difficulty in giving up what one does not hold with cupidity. And indeed those men knew that in their marriages intemperate lechery was to be avoided, as the prayer made by Tobias when he was joined to a wife testifies. For he said: "Lord God of our fathers, may the heavens and the earth, and the sea, and the fountains, and the rivers, and all thy creatures that are in them, bless thee. Thou madest Adam of the slime of the earth, and gavest him Eve for a

[1] 1 Cor. 7. 2, 6.   [2] Cf. Eccles. 3. 5.

helper. And now, Lord, thou knowest, that not for fleshly lust do I take my sister to wife, but because of truth itself, that thou mayest have mercy on us, O Lord." [3]

XIX

28. Those who have given the reins to libido, either wandering about in abandonment among many whoredoms or in a single marriage itself not only exceeding the measure necessary to the procreation of children but also accumulating stains of inhuman intemperance with the completely shameless license of a certain servile liberty, do not believe it possible that men of old could use many women temperately, seeking nothing in that use but the office of propagation, as was appropriate in those times. And since they who are caught in snares of libido do not behave in this way with one wife, they think it could not be done in any way with many.

29. Moreover, these men might say that it is not proper to honor and to praise good and holy men, because when they themselves are honored and praised they swell with pride; they become more avid for the most empty glory the more often and the more thoroughly they are fanned by a flattering tongue. They become so light that a breath of rumor, whether they think it favorable or unfavorable, blows them into whirlpools of vices or casts them against rocks of crimes. Let them see, therefore, how laborious and difficult it is for them neither to be lured by the bait of praise nor to be penetrated by the stings of contumely. But let them not measure others by themselves.

XX

Rather they should believe that our Apostles were neither inflated when they were admired by men nor cast down when they were despised. Indeed, those men lacked neither temptation, for they were celebrated by the praise of believers and de-

---

[3] Cf. Tob. 8. 7-9. The end of the passage is changed to follow St. Augustine's text.

famed by the curses of persecutors. And just as they used these things in accordance with the circumstances, so the men of old, referring the use of women to the circumstances of their time, did not suffer that domination of libido which is served by those who do not believe these things.

30. If the men of old had fallen into any such domination they could not have restrained an inexpiable hatred of their sons by whom they knew their wives and concubines to have been tempted or seduced.

XXI

For King David, when he suffered this evil from his impious and monstrous son, not only tolerated his madness but even lamented his death.[1] He was not held ensnared by carnal jealousy since he was not moved at all by the injury to himself but only by the sin of his son. Thus he ordered that he be not killed when he was captured so that he might have an opportunity to repent after he had been subdued. And when this proved impossible, he did not lament his bereavement at the boy's death; he sorrowed because he knew into what pains such an impious, adulterous, and parricidal soul would be swept away. And he was joyful at the earlier death of a son who was innocent, after he had been distressed because of his sickness.[2]

31. The following incident demonstrates the moderation and temperance with which these men used their wives. When this same king illicitly seized a woman, being swept up in the passion of youth and temporal prosperity, even ordering that her husband be killed, he was accused by a prophet. When the prophet came to him to make him recognize his sin, he proposed to him a similitude of a poor man who had one lamb. His neighbor, although he had many sheep, offered a guest of his the single small lamb of his poor neighbor as a feast. Moved by this story, David ordered the rich man to be killed and the lamb of the poor man to be restored fourfold,

[1] 2 Kings [2 Sam.] 18. 33.   [2] 2 Kings [2 Sam.] 12. 16-23.

so that he who had sinned knowingly condemned himself un-
knowingly. When this had been made clear to him, and the
divine punishment demonstrated, he expiated his sin in
penance.[3] However, in this similitude the adultery only is
signified in the lamb of the poor man. Concerning the mur-
dered husband of the woman, that is, concerning the death of
the poor man who had only one lamb, David was not questioned by similitude, so that his sentence of condemnation
speaks only of adultery. From this account it should be understood with what temperance he had many wives when concerning one for whom he exceeded the bounds of moderation he
was forced to punish himself. But in this man immoderate
libido was not a permanent but a passing thing, so that in the
argument of the prophet illicit appetite is called a guest. He
did not say that he offered the lamb of the poor man as a
feast to his king but to his guest. However, in his son Solomon
libido was not a passing guest; it reigned as a king. Scripture
does not pass this over in silence, but blames him as a lover of
women.[4] His beginnings were redolent with the desire for
wisdom; [5] when he had obtained it through spiritual love, he
lost it through carnal love.

XXII

32. Therefore, although all or almost all of the deeds which
are contained in the Old Testament are to be taken figuratively as well as literally, nevertheless the reader may take as
literal those performed by people who are praised, even
though they would be abhorrent to the custom of the good
who follow the divine precepts after the advent of the Lord.
He should refer the figure to the understanding, but should
not transfer the deed itself to his own mores. Many things
were done in the course of duty in those times which now
cannot be done without libidinousness.

---

3 2 Kings [2 Sam.] 12. 1-14.   5 2 Par. [2 Chron.] 1. 7-12.
4 3 Kings [1 Kings] 11. 1.

XXIII

33. If he reads of the sins of great men, even though he can see and verify in them figures of future things, he may put the nature of the things done to this use, that he will never hear himself boast of his own virtuous deeds and condemn others from the vantage of his righteousness when he sees in such men the tempests that are to be shunned and the ship-wrecks that are to be lamented. The sins of these men have been recorded for a reason, and that is that the lesson of the Apostle may be everywhere momentous, where he says, "He that thinketh himself to stand, let him take heed lest he fall." [1] There is hardly a page in the holy books in which it is not shown that God resists the proud but to the humble offers grace.[2]

XXIV

34. Thus it is of the first importance that we determine whether or not a passage which we wish to understand is figurative. If it is determined that it is figurative, it is easy to examine it in every way, having applied the rules concerning things which we have discussed in the first book, until we come to the lesson of truth, especially when piety assists a practice fortified by effort. We can discover whether an expression is literal or figurative in accordance with these things which have been said above.

XXV

When a figurative locution appears, the words of which it is composed will be seen to be derived from similar things or related to such things by some association.

35. But since things are similar to other things in a great many ways, we must not think it to be prescribed that what a thing signifies by similitude in one place must always be

1 1 Cor. 10. 12.
2 Cf. Prov. 3. 34; Jas. 4. 6; 1 Pet. 5. 5.

signified by that thing. For the Lord used "leaven" in vituperation when He said, "Beware of the leaven of the Pharisees," [1] and in praise when He said, "The kingdom of God . . . is like to leaven, which a woman took and hid in three measures of meal, till the whole was leavened." [2]

36. This variation takes two forms. Thus one thing signifies another thing and still another either in such a way that the second thing signified is contrary to the first or in such a way that the second thing is entirely different from the first. The things signified are contrary, that is, when one thing is used as a similitude in a good sense and in another place in an evil sense, like "leaven" in the above example. This is the situation where the lion is used to signify Christ, when it is said, "The lion of the tribe of Juda . . . has prevailed," [3] but also signifies the Devil, when it is written, "Your adversary the devil, as a roaring lion, goeth about seeking whom he may devour." [4] Thus the serpent appears in a good sense in "wise as serpents," [5] but in a bad sense in "the serpent seduced Eve by his subtilty." [6] Bread is used in a good sense in "I am the living bread which came down from heaven," [7] but in a bad sense in "hidden bread is more pleasant." [8] Many other things are used in the same way. Those examples which I have mentioned create little doubt as to their meaning, for things ought not to be used as examples unless they are clear. There are, however, instances in which it is uncertain whether the signification is to be taken in a good sense or in an evil sense, like "in the hand of the Lord there is a cup of strong wine full of mixture." It is uncertain whether this may signify the wrath of God but not to the ultimate penalty, or, that is, "the dregs," or whether it may signify rather the grace of the Scriptures passing from the Jews to the Gentiles, because "he hath poured it out from this to that," certain practices remaining among the Jews which they understand carnally because "the dregs

1 Matt. 16. 11.   5 Matt. 10. 16.
2 Luke 13. 20-21.   6 2 Cor. 11. 3.
3 Apoc. 5. 5.   7 John 6. 51.
4 1 Pet. 5. 8.   8 Prov. 9. 17.

thereof are not emptied." [1] To show that one thing may have significations which are not contrary but diverse, we may use as an example the fact that water is used in the Apocalypse to signify people,[2] but it also signifies the Holy Spirit, as in "out of his belly shall flow rivers of living water." [3] And thus water may be seen to signify one thing and another in accordance with the passages in which it is used.

37. In the same way other things signify not one thing but more, and not only two diverse things, but sometimes many different things in accordance with the meaning of passages in which they are found.

XXVI

In those places where things are used openly we may learn how to interpret them when they appear in obscure places. In no better way may we understand what is said to God in "Take hold of arms and shield: and rise up to help me" [4] than by consulting that passage which reads, "O Lord, thou hast crowned us, as with a shield of thy good will." [5] But we should not pursue this practice in such a way that everywhere we read of a shield raised for defense we should think of nothing except the good will of God; for it is also said that there is "the shield of faith, wherewith you may be able to extinguish all the fiery darts of the most wicked one." [6] Nor again with reference to this kind of spiritual armor must we attribute faith to the shield alone, since in another place the breastplate is said to be faith: "having on," he says, "the breastplate of faith and charity." [7]

XXVII

38. When, however, from a single passage in the Scripture not one but two or more meanings are elicited, even if what he who wrote the passage intended remains hidden, there is no

1 Ps. 74. 9 [75. 8].
2 Apoc. 17. 15; 19. 6.
3 John 7. 38.
4 Ps. 34. 2 [35. 2].

5 Ps. 5. 13 [5. 12].
6 Eph. 6. 16.
7 1 Thess. 5. 8.

danger if any of the meanings may be seen to be congruous
with the truth taught in other passages of the Holy Scriptures.
For he who examines the divine eloquence, desiring to discover the intention of the author through whom the Holy
Spirit created the Scripture, whether he attains this end or
finds another meaning in the words not contrary to right
faith, is free from blame if he has evidence from some other
place in the divine books. For the author himself may have
seen the same meaning in the words we seek to understand.
And certainly the Spirit of God, who worked through that
author, undoubtedly foresaw that this meaning would occur
to the reader or listener. Rather, He provided that it might
occur to him, since that meaning is dependent upon truth.
For what could God have more generously and abundantly
provided in the divine writings than that the same words
might be understood in various ways which other no less
divine witnesses approve?

XXVIII

39. However, when a meaning is elicited whose uncertainty
cannot be resolved by the evidence of places in the Scriptures
whose meaning is certain, it remains to make it more clear by
recourse to reason, even if he whose words we seek to understand did not perhaps intend that meaning. But this is a
dangerous pursuit; we shall walk much more safely with the
aid of the Scriptures themselves. When we wish to examine
passages obscured by figurative words, we should either begin
with a passage which is not controversial, or, if it is controversial, we should conclude with testimonies applied from
places wherever they are found in the same Scriptures.

XXIX

40. Lettered men should know, moreover, that all those
modes of expression which the grammarians designate with
the Greek word *tropes* were used by our authors, and more
abundantly and copiously than those who do not know them

and have learned about such expressions elsewhere are able
to suppose or believe. Those who know these tropes, however,
will recognize them in the sacred letters, and this knowledge
will be of considerable assistance in understanding them. But
it is not proper to teach them to the ignorant here, lest we
seem to be teaching the art of grammar. I advise that they be
learned elsewhere, although I have already advised the same
thing before in the second book where I discussed the necessary knowledge of languages. For letters from which grammar
takes its name—the Greeks call letters *grámmata*—are indeed
signs of sounds made by the articulate voice with which we
speak. And not only examples of all of these tropes are found
in reading the sacred books, but also the names of some of
them, like *allegoria, aenigma, parabola.* And yet almost all of
these tropes, said to be learned in the liberal arts, find a place
in the speech of those who have never heard the lectures of
grammarians and are content with the usage of common
speech. For who does not say, "So may you flourish"? And this
is the trope called metaphor. Who does not use the word
piscina [basin, pool, pond, tank, or other large container for
water] for something which neither contains fish nor was constructed for the use of fish, when the word itself is derived
from *piscis* [fish]? This trope is called catachresis.

41. It would be tedious to describe other examples of this
kind. For the vulgar speech even extends to those tropes
which are more remarkable because they imply the opposite
of what is said, like that which is called irony or antiphrasis.
Now irony indicates by inflection what it wishes to be understood, as when we say to a man who is doing evil, "You are
doing well." Antiphrasis, however, does not rely on inflection
that it may signify the contrary, but either uses its own words
whose origin is from the contrary, like *lucus,* "grove," so
called *quod minime luceat,* "because it has very little light";
or it indicates that a thing is so when it wishes to imply the
contrary, as when we seek to obtain what is not there and we
are told, "There is plenty." Or, by adding words we may indicate that what we say is to be taken in a contrary sense, as

when we say, "Beware of him, for he is a good man." And
what unlearned man does not say such things without knowing at all what these tropes are or what they are called? Yet
an awareness of them is necessary to a solution of the ambiguities of the Scriptures, for when the sense is absurd if it is
taken verbally, it is to be inquired whether or not what is
said is expressed in this or that trope which we do not know;
and in this way many hidden things are discovered.

XXX

42. A certain Tyconius who wrote most triumphantly
against the Donatists, although he himself was a Donatist and
hence is found to have had an absurd mentality where he did
not wish to abandon them altogether, wrote a book which he
called *Of Rules,*[1] since in it he explained seven rules with
which, as if with keys, the obscurities of the Divine Scriptures
might be opened. Of these the first is "Of the Lord and His
Body," the second "Of the Bipartite Body of the Lord," the
third "Of Promises and the Law," the fourth "Of Species and
Genus," the fifth "Of Times," the sixth "Of Recapitulation,"
the seventh "Of the Devil and his Body." When these are
examined as he explains them, they are of no little assistance
in penetrating what is covert in the Holy Scriptures. However,
not all the things which are so written that they are difficult
to understand may be cleared up by means of these rules, and
many other methods must be used which he was so far from
including in this series of seven that he himself explains many
obscure places without recourse to them because they do not
apply. For example, none of them was used or brought in
question when he sought to discover how we should understand in the Apocalypse of St. John the seven angels of the
churches to whom John is commanded to write.[2] He reasons
in many ways and concludes that by the angels we should
understand the churches. But in this copious disputation none

[1] See F. C. Burkitt, *The Rules of Tyconious* (Cambridge, 1894).
[2] Apoc. 1. 20.

of these rules is employed, although the matter inquired into is very obscure. Enough has been said by way of example, for to collect all the examples of places in the Scriptures which are obscure in such a way that no one of these seven rules applies would be too laborious and tedious.

43. But when Tyconius commended these principles as rules, he attributed such virtue to them that they would help us to understand almost all those things which are said obcurely in the Law, or in the divine books, provided that we understood them and knew how to apply them. He introduced his book with these words: "I thought it necessary before all the other matters which occurred to me to write a book of Rules, and to fabricate, as it were, keys and windows for the secrets of the Law. For there are certain mystic rules which reveal what is hidden in the whole Law and make visible the treasures of truth which are invisible to some. If the sense of these rules is accepted without envy as we have explained it, whatever is closed will be opened, and whatever is obscure will be illuminated, so that he who walks through the immense forest of prophecy led by these rules as if by pathways of light will be defended from error." If he had said here, "There are certain mystic rules which reveal what is hidden in some of the Law," or, indeed, "in much of the Law," and not "in the whole Law," as he put it, and if he had not said, "Whatever is closed will be opened," but "Much that is closed will be opened," he would have spoken the truth. Nor would he have given his reader and judge false hope by attributing too much to such an elaborate and useful work. I thought that this should be said so that this book, which is of great assistance in understanding the Scriptures, might be read by students in such a way that they do not expect from it that which it does not have to offer. Indeed, it is to be read cautiously, not only because of certain things in which he erred as a man, but especially because he wrote as a Donatist heretic. I shall explain very briefly what these seven rules may teach or admonish.

XXXI

44. The first is "Of the Lord and His Body," according to which it is understood that sometimes the head and the body, that is, Christ and the Church, are indicated to us as one person (nor was it in vain said to the faithful, "Then are you the seed of Abraham,"[1] when there is one seed of Abraham, who is Christ), and we should not hesitate when the discussion moves from the head to the body or from the body to the head without leaving the subject of the single person. Thus one person is speaking in "as a bridegroom decked with a crown, and as a bride adorned with her jewels,"[2] but which of the two applies to the head and which to the body, that is, which applies to Christ and which applies to the Church, should be understood.

XXXII

45. The second is "Of the Bipartite Body of the Lord," which should not be designated in that way since that is not actually the body of the Lord which will not be with Him in eternity. Rather it should be called "Of the True and Mixed Body of the Lord," or "the True and Simulated," or something else, because hypocrites should not be said to be with Him either in eternity or even now, although they seem to be in His Church. Whence this rule might have been named in such a way that it designated the "mixed Church." This rule requires a vigilant reader when the Scripture seems to speak to or about persons to or about whom it was just speaking but actually speaks to or about other persons as if all of these persons were of one body because of association in time and participation in the Sacraments. These words in the Canticle pertain to this: "I am black but beautiful . . . as the tents of Cedar, as the curtains of Solomon."[1] She does not say, "I *was* black as the tents of Cedar, and I *am* beautiful as the curtains of Solomon"; but she says that she is both because of the

[1] Gal. 3. 29.   [2] Isa. 61. 10.   [1] Cant. 1. 4 [Song of Sol. 1. 5].

temporal unity of good and bad fish within a single net.[2] For the tents of Cedar pertain to Ismael, who "shall not be heir with the son of the freewoman." [3] Thus when God says concerning the good part: "And I will lead the blind into the way which they know not: and in the paths which they were ignorant of I will make them walk: I will make darkness light before them and crooked things straight: these things have I done to them, and have not forsaken them," [4] He immediately turns to the other part mixed with evil and says, "They are turned back," [5] as if those already spoken about were referred to in these words. But since they are for a time together, they are spoken of as though they were the ones already spoken of; but they will not always be in one body. For among them is that servant remembered in the Gospel, whose master, when he comes, "shall separate him, and appoint his portion with the hypocrites." [6]

XXXIII

46. The third rule is "Of Promises and the Law," which may be spoken of in another way, "Concerning the Spirit and the Letter," as we called it when we composed a book on the subject. It may also be called "Of Grace and Commandment." But this seems to me to be a great question rather than a rule to be used in solving other questions. It is on account of a failure to understand this that the Pelagians constitute or support their heresy. Tyconius labors well but not at length in the solution of this problem. Speaking of faith and works, he said that works were given to us by God because of the merit of faith; but faith, he said, originates in us and is not a gift of God. He had not listened to the Apostle, who said, "Peace be to the brethren and charity with faith, from God the Father, and the Lord Jesus Christ." [1] But he was not familiar with that heresy which has grown up in our times and has exercised many of us so that we have defended against its attacks the

2 Matt. 13. 47-48.
3 Gal. 4. 30, from Gen. 21. 10.
4 Isa. 42. 16.
5 Isa. 42. 17.
6 Matt. 24. 51.
1 Eph. 6. 23.

grace of God which has come to us through Our Lord Jesus Christ. According to the words of the Apostle, "There must also be heresies: that they also, who are approved, may be made manifest among you." [2] This heresy has rendered us much more vigilant and diligent so that we attend to those things in the sacred Scriptures which were overlooked by Tyconius, who, being without an enemy, was less attentive, neglecting among other things the fact that faith is the gift of Him who has divided to everyone his measure of it.[3] On the basis of this principle it was said to certain persons, "For unto you it is given for Christ, not only to believe in him, but also to suffer for him." [4] How can one doubt that they are both gifts of God if he faithfully and intelligently hears that they were given? There are many other testimonies to the same thing, but we are not discussing this subject now, although we have discussed it frequently in other places.

XXXIV

47. The fourth rule of Tyconius is "Of Species and Genus." He calls it this, wishing to understand by the "species" the part and by the "genus" the whole whose part is that which is called the "species," just as a city, which he calls the "species," is a part of the whole world of men, which he calls "genus." Nor do we have to apply here that subtlety taught by the dialecticians who dispute most acutely the difference between a part and a species. The same relationship applies if we discover anything in the Sacred Scriptures concerning, not a single city, but a single province or people or kingdom. For example, it is not only concerning Jerusalem, or some city of the Gentiles, either Tyre, Babylon, or some other city, that things are said in the Sacred Scriptures which apply beyond the bounds of those cities and are applicable rather to all peoples. Indeed, in the same way, things are said concerning Judea, Egypt, Assyria, and other nations, in which there are many

[2] 1 Cor. 11. 19.   [4] Phil. 1. 29.
[3] Cf. Rom. 12. 3.

cities, which are not the whole world but only a part of it, but
which apply to the whole race of men of which they are a part,
or, as Tyconius calls it, to the "genus" of which these nations
are "species." These words have come into common usage in
this sense, so that even the uneducated understand what is to
apply generally and what is to apply specially in any imperial
edict. The same sort of thing happens with reference to men,
so that things said about Solomon exceed the bounds of special
application to him, but become clear when they are related to
Christ or to the Church of which he is a part.

48. The application to the species is not always exceeded;
frequently things are said which apply to it as well or most
clearly apply only to it. But when a transition is made from
the species to the genus, as happens sometimes when the Scripture has been considering the species for some time, the reader
should maintain a vigilant attitude lest he seek in the species
what may be better and more certainly found in the genus.
It is easy to understand what the prophet Ezechiel said:
"When the house of Israel dwelt in their own land, they
defiled it with their ways, and with their doings: their way was
before me like the uncleanness of a menstruous woman. And
I poured out my indignation upon them for the blood which
they had shed upon the land, and with their idols they defiled it. And I scattered them among the nations, and they are
dispersed through the countries: I have judged them according
to their ways and their devices." [1] It is easy, I say, to understand this as it applies to that house of Israel of which the
Apostle says, "Behold Israel according to the flesh," [2] because
the carnal people of Israel did these things and suffered these
things. And other things which follow may also be applied to
that same people. But when the prophet begins to say, "And
I will sanctify my great name, which was profaned among the
Gentiles, which you have profaned in the midst of them: that
the Gentiles may know that I am the Lord," then he who reads
should be aware of the way in which the species is exceeded
and the genus is added. For he continues and says: "And when

1 Ezech. [Ezek.] 36. 17-19.   2 1 Cor. 10. 18.

I shall be sanctified in you before their eyes . . . I will take you from among the Gentiles and will gather you together out of all the countries, and will bring you into your own land. And I will pour upon you clean water, and you shall be cleansed from all your filthiness, and I will cleanse you from all your idols. And I will give you a new heart, and put a new spirit within you: and I will take away the stony heart out of your flesh, and will give you a heart of flesh. And I will put my spirit in the midst of you: and I will cause you to walk in my commandments, and to keep my judgments, and do them. And you shall dwell in the land which I gave to your fathers, and you shall be my people, and I will be your God. And I will save you from all your uncleannesses." [3] This was prophesied of the New Testament, to which pertains not only that one race in its remnant of which it is said elsewhere, "If the number of the children of Israel be as the sand of the sea, a remnant shall be saved," [4] but also other people, whose fathers, who are also our fathers, received promise. No one who reads this passage doubts that the "laver of regeneration," [5] which we now see given to all peoples, is here promised. And that which the Apostle said when he commended the grace of the New Testament so that it is eminent with respect to the Old—"You are our epistle, written in our hearts . . . written not with ink, but with the spirit of the living God; not in tables of stone, but in the fleshly tables of the heart" [6]—is seen to look back to this and to be derived from the passage where the prophet says: "And I will give you a new heart, and put a new spirit within you: and I will take away the stony heart out of your flesh, and will give you a heart of flesh." By the "heart of flesh," whence the Apostle derived "the fleshly tables of the heart," he wished to distinguish the sentient life, and by the sentient life he signified understanding. Thus the spiritual Israel becomes not one people but all to whose fathers there was promise in their seed, which is Christ.

3 Ezech. [Ezek.] 36. 23-29.   5 Titus 3. 5.
4 Rom. 9. 27, from Isa. 10. 22.   6 2 Cor. 3. 2-3.

49. Therefore this spiritual Israel is to be distinguished from that carnal Israel which is one people by newness of grace, not by nobility of descent, by their minds and not by their race. But the high prophetic style, when it speaks to the carnal Israel or about it, secretly moves to the spiritual, and when it speaks now of one and now of the other, it seems to be confusing them, not that it envies us an understanding of the Scriptures, but in order to provide a medicinal exercise. Whence also that which says, "I will bring you into your own land," and a little later, as if repeating itself, "And you shall dwell in the land which I gave to thy fathers," must be taken, not carnally to refer to the carnal Israel, but spiritually, to refer to the spiritual Israel. Indeed, the Church, "not having spot or wrinkle," [7] made up of all peoples and reigning with Christ eternally, is itself the land of the blessed, "the land of the living." [8] This, we must understand, was given to our fathers when it was promised to them by the certain and immutable will of God, for, by the firmness of the promise or prophecy, that was already given which our fathers thought was to be given in its own time. Thus the Apostle, writing to Timothy, says of the grace given to the saints: "Not according to our works, but according to his own purpose and grace, which was given us in Christ Jesus before the times of the world: But is now made manifest by the illumination of our Saviour Jesus Christ." [9] He says that grace was given when there were not yet those to whom it could be given, for in the disposition and predestination of God that was already done which in its own time was yet to come and which, he says, is now manifest. Moreover, these things may be understood also of the future age when there shall be "a new heaven and a new earth" [10] in which the unjust will not be able to dwell. And thus it is rightly said to the pious that this will be their land, of which no part will be for the impious, since it too was similarly given when the giving was confirmed.

[7] Eph. 5. 27.
[8] Ps. 26. 13 [27. 13].

[9] 2 Tim. 1. 9-10.
[10] Apoc. 21. 1.

XXXV

50. Tyconius sets forth a fifth rule which he calls "Of Times," with which intervals of time which are hidden in the Scriptures may frequently be discovered or conjectured. However, he says that this rule operates in two ways, either by the trope of synecdoche or by "legitimate" numbers. The trope of synecdoche causes us to understand either a part from the whole or the whole from a part. Thus one Evangelist says that a thing was done after eight days which another says was done after six days when on the mountain before only three disciples the face of the Lord shone like the sun and his garments became white as snow.[1] Both things which were said about the number of days could not be true unless he who said "after eight days" is understood to have counted the last part of the day on which Christ foretold what was to come and the first part of the day on which he showed it fulfilled as two whole days. But he who said "after six days" should be understood to have counted whole and complete days. This method of speaking, by which the whole is signified by the part, also solves a question about the Resurrection of Christ. For unless the latter part of the day on which He suffered is considered a whole day, the previous night being added, and unless the night in whose last part He arose is taken as a whole day, adding, that is, the dawning Lord's Day, there can be no way of computing the three days and three nights during which He predicted that He would be "in the heart of the earth." [2]

51. He calls those numbers "legitimate" which Divine Scripture commends above others, like seven, ten, twelve, and others which the studious reader will easily recognize. Many numbers of this kind are used for time as a whole, whence "seven times a day I have given praise to thee" [3] means the same thing as "always his praise shall be in my mouth." [4]

[1] Matt. 17. 1-2; Mark 9. 2-3; Luke 9. 28-29.
[2] Matt. 12. 40.   [4] Ps. 33. 2 [34. 1].
[3] Ps. 118. 164 [119. 164].

They have the same meaning when they are multiplied by ten, like seventy and seven hundred, whence the seventy years of Jeremias [5] may be spiritually interpreted to mean the whole time during which the Church is among strangers. The same holds true if these numbers are multiplied by themselves, as ten tens are a hundred, and twelve twelves are a hundred and forty-four, a number which signifies all of the faithful in the Apocalypse.[6] Whence it appears that these numbers are of value not only for solving questions of time but that their significances are broad and touch on many things. Nor does this number in the Apocalypse apply to times, but to men.

XXXVI

- 52. Tyconius calls the sixth rule "Recapitulation," discovered in the obscurity of the Scriptures with no little vigilance. Some things are so described as though they follow each other in the order of time, or as if they narrate a continuous sequence of events, when the narrative covertly refers to previous events which had been omitted; and unless this situation is understood in accordance with this rule, the reader will err. For example, we read in Genesis: "And the Lord God had planted a paradise of pleasure [in Eden toward the East] wherein he placed man whom he had formed. And the Lord God brought forth of the ground all manner of trees fair to behold, and pleasant to eat of." [1] This last seems to be said in such a way as to indicate that it was done after God had placed man in Paradise. When both things have been mentioned briefly, that is, that God planted Paradise and placed man whom he had formed in it, the narrative by recapitulation returns and indicates what was passed over, that is, the manner in which Paradise was planted when "God brought forth of the ground all manner of trees fair to behold, and pleasant to eat of." Then this is added: "the tree of life also in the midst of paradise: and the tree of knowledge of

5 Jer. 25. 11.   1 Gen. 2. 8-9.
6 Apoc. 7. 4.

good and evil." Then the river by which paradise is irrigated, divided into four heads of four streams, is explained, all of which pertains to the creation of paradise. When the writer has completed this, he repeats what he has already said concerning what actually followed, saying, "And the Lord God took man, and put him into the paradise of pleasure," [2] and so on. For after these things had been done man was placed there, as the order of the narrative now demonstrates. These things pertaining to the creation of Paradise were not done after man was placed there, as what was first said may be taken to mean unless the recapitulation by which it refers to things omitted earlier is understood by the vigilant reader.

53. Again in the same book when the generations of the sons of Noah are discussed, it is said, "These are the children of Cham in their kindreds, and tongues, and generations, and lands, and nations." And when the children of Sem are enumerated it is said, "These are the children of Sem according to their kindreds and tongues and countries in their nations." And it is added concerning all of them, "These are the families of Noe, according to their peoples and nations. By these were the nations divided on the earth after the flood. And the earth was of one tongue, and of the same speech." [3] And because this was included, "And the earth was of one tongue, and of the same speech," that is, with one language for all, it seems to be said that at that time when they had been dispersed over the earth according to their peoples and nations there was a common language for all. And this without doubt contradicts the earlier statements where they are said to be divided into their nations according to their tongues. Nor could it be said that the single nations had their own tongues which made them separate peoples when there was one language for all of them. But this passage is added by recapitulation, "And the earth was of one tongue, and of one speech," since in it the narrative goes back subtly so that it

2 Gen. 2. 15.   3 Gen. 10. 20, 31, 32; 11. 1.

may be explained how it came about that the people who had a common language were divided by many; and immediately the narration proceeds to an account of the building of that tower where this punishment for pride was administered by divine judgment, after which they were dispersed over the earth according to their various tongues.

54. This recapitulation may be made more obscure, as when the Lord says in the Gospel: "And in the day that Lot went out of Sodom, it rained fire and brimstone from heaven, and destroyed them all. Even thus shall it be in the day when the Son of man shall be revealed. In that hour, he that shall be on the housetop, and his goods in the house, let him not go down to take them away: and he that shall be in the field, in like manner, let him not return back. Remember Lot's wife." [4] Is it when the Lord shall be revealed that these commandments are to be observed lest anyone look back, that is, seek the past life which he has renounced, or, rather, is it at this present time that a man should obey them so that when the Lord shall be revealed he may find retribution for those things which he has observed or scorned? Since it is said "in that hour," it might be thought that these things are to be observed then, when the Lord shall be revealed, unless the mind of the reader is awake to an understanding of recapitulation, assisted by another Scripture which in the time of the Apostles themselves announced, "Little children, it is the last hour." [5] Therefore the time in which the gospel was preached extending to the time in which the Lord shall be revealed is the hour during which these commands are to be observed, for the revelation of the Lord itself pertains to that same hour which shall be terminated by the Day of Judgment.

XXXVII

55. The seventh rule of Tyconius, and the last, is "Of the Devil and his Body." For he is the head of the impious, who

4 Luke 17. 29-32.   5 1 John 2. 18.

are in a way his body, and who will go with him to the tortures of eternal fire [1] in the same way that Christ is the head of the Church, which is His body, and will be with Him in His Kingdom and everlasting glory. Therefore, just as in the first rule called "Of the Lord and His Body" it is necessary to be alert in order to understand what pertains to the head and what pertains to the body when the Scripture speaks of one and the same person, so in this last one, sometimes things are said concerning the Devil which may be understood not with reference to himself, but rather to his body. This body is not only made up of those who are manifestly "without," [2] but also of those who, although they belong to it, for a time mingle with the Church until each one of them leaves this life, or until the fan shall at last separate the wheat from the chaff.[3] That which is written in Isaias, "How art thou fallen from heaven, O Lucifer, who didst rise in the morning?" [4] and the other things which are said under the figure of the king of Babylon concerning the same person or to the same person in the same context, are certainly all to be understood concerning the Devil; and yet when it is said, "How art thou fallen to the earth, that didst wound the nations?",[5] the idea does not totally apply to the head. For although the Devil sends his angels to all the nations, nevertheless his body, rather than himself, is cast down upon the earth, except in that he is in his body which is crushed "like the dust, which the wind driveth from the face of the earth." [6]

56. All of these rules except one, which is called "Of Promises and the Law," cause one thing to be understood from another, a situation proper to figurative locutions. The scope of such expressions, it seems to me, is too broad for any one man to comprehend entirely. For wherever one wishes to say one thing so that another is understood, even though the name of the particular trope employed is not found in the art of rhetoric, he uses a figurative expression. When such ex-

[1] Cf. Matt. 25. 41.   [4] Isa. 14. 12.
[2] 1 Cor. 5. 12.   [5] Isa. 14. 12.
[3] Cf. Luke 3. 17.   [6] Ps. 1. 4.

pressions are found in accustomed places, the mind follows them without difficulty; when they are in unexpected places, labor is necessary to understand them, more for some and less for others, as the gifts of God are greater or less in the minds of men, or as they have greater or less assistance. Accordingly, just as with reference to literal expressions which we have discussed above, where things are to be understood as they are spoken, so also with reference to figurative expressions where one thing is understood by another, we have done as much as seems sufficient. Students of the Holy Scriptures are not only to be admonished that they know the kinds of expression that are used there, and that they observe vigilantly and hold by memory the manner in which things are customarily said there, but also, and this is most important, that they pray for understanding. For in these books concerning which they are studious they read that "the Lord giveth wisdom: and out of his mouth cometh prudence and knowledge." [7] They have also received from Him their desire for study, if it is upheld by piety. But enough has been said concerning signs, in so far as the subject pertains to words. It remains that we set forth in the following book what the Lord has provided us concerning the manner of expressing what is thought.

BOOK FOUR

1. This work of ours entitled *On Christian Doctrine* was at the beginning divided into two parts. For after the Prologue in which I replied to those who would criticize it, I wrote, "There are two things necessary to the treatment of the Scriptures: a way of discovering those things which are to be understood, and a way of teaching what we have learned. We shall speak first of discovery and second of teaching." Since

[7] Prov. 2. 6.

we have already said much concerning discovery and devoted three books to that one part, with the help of God we shall say a few things concerning teaching, so that, if possible, we shall conclude everything with one book and thus complete the whole work in four books.

I

2. But first in these preliminary remarks I must thwart the expectation of those readers who think that I shall give the rules of rhetoric here which I learned and taught in the secular schools. And I admonish them not to expect such rules from me, not that they have no utility, but because, if they have any, it should be sought elsewhere if perhaps some good man has the opportunity to learn them. But he should not expect these rules from me, either in this work or in any other.

II

3. For since by means of the art of rhetoric both truth and falsehood are urged, who would dare to say that truth should stand in the person of its defenders unarmed against lying, so that they who wish to urge falsehoods may know how to make their listeners benevolent, or attentive, or docile in their presentation, while the defenders of truth are ignorant of that art? Should they speak briefly, clearly, and plausibly while the defenders of truth speak so that they tire their listeners, make themselves difficult to understand and what they have to say dubious? Should they oppose the truth with fallacious arguments and assert falsehoods, while the defenders of truth have no ability either to defend the truth or to oppose the false? Should they, urging the minds of their listeners into error, ardently exhort them, moving them by speech so that they terrify, sadden, and exhilarate them, while the defenders of truth are sluggish, cold, and somnolent? Who is so foolish as to think this to be wisdom? While the faculty of eloquence, which is of great value in urging either evil or justice, is in itself indifferent, why should it not be obtained for the uses of

the good in the service of truth if the evil usurp it for the winning of perverse and vain causes in defense of iniquity and error?

III

4. But whatever observations and rules concerning this matter there may be, in accordance with which one acquires through exercise and habit a most skillful use of vocabulary and plentiful verbal ornaments, are established by what is called eloquence or oratory. Those who are able to do so quickly, having set aside an appropriate period of time, should learn them at a proper and convenient age outside of these writings of mine. For the masters of Roman eloquence themselves did not hesitate to say that, unless one can learn this art quickly, he can hardly learn it at all. Why should we inquire whether this is true? For even if these rules can sometimes be learned by those who are slow, we do not hold them to be of such importance that we would wish mature and grave men to spend their time learning them. It is enough that they be the concern of youths; nor should they concern all of those whom we wish to educate for the utility of the Church, but only those who are not pursuing some more urgent study, or one which obviously ought to take precedence over this one. For those with acute and eager minds more readily learn eloquence by reading and hearing the eloquent than by following the rules of eloquence. There is no lack of ecclesiastical literature, including that outside of the canon established in a place of secure authority, which, if read by a capable man, even though he is interested more in what is said than in the eloquence with which it is said, will imbue him with that eloquence while he is studying. And he will learn eloquence especially if he gains practice by writing, dictating, or speaking what he has learned according to the rule of piety and faith. But if capacity of this kind to learn eloquence is lacking, the rules of rhetoric will not be understood, nor will it help any if they are in some small measure understood after great labor. Even those who have learned these rules and speak fluently and elo-

quently cannot be aware of the fact that they are applying them while they are speaking unless they are discussing the rules themselves; indeed, I think that there is hardly a single eloquent man who can both speak well and think of the rules of eloquence while he is speaking. And we should beware lest what should be said escape us while we are thinking of the artistry of the discourse. Moreover, in the speeches and sayings of the eloquent, the precepts of eloquence are found to have been fulfilled, although the speakers did not think of them in order to be eloquent or while they were being eloquent, and they were eloquent whether they had learned the rules or never come in contact with them. They fulfilled them because they were eloquent; they did not apply them that they might be eloquent.

5. Therefore, since infants are not taught to speak except by learning the expressions of speakers, why can men not be made eloquent, not by teaching them the rules of eloquence, but by having them read and hear the expressions of the eloquent and imitate them in so far as they are able to follow them? Have we not seen examples of this being done? For we know many men ignorant of the rules of eloquence who are more eloquent than many who have learned them; but we know of no one who is eloquent without having read or heard the disputations and sayings of the eloquent. For boys do not need the art of grammar which teaches correct speech if they have the opportunity to grow up and live among men who speak correctly. Without knowing any of the names of the errors, they criticize and avoid anything erroneous they hear spoken on the basis of their own habits of speech, just as city dwellers, even if they are illiterate, criticize the speech of rustics.

IV

6. Thus the expositor and teacher of the Divine Scripture, the defender of right faith and the enemy of error, should both teach the good and extirpate the evil. And in this labor of words, he should conciliate those who are opposed, arouse

those who are remiss, and teach those ignorant of his subject what is occurring and what they should expect. But when he has either found his listeners to be benevolent, attentive, and docile, or has caused them to be so, other aims are to be carried out as the cause requires. If those who hear are to be taught, exposition must be composed, if it is needed, that they may become acquainted with the subject at hand. In order that those things which are doubtful may be made certain, they must be reasoned out with the use of evidence. But if those who hear are to be moved rather than taught, so that they may not be sluggish in putting what they know into practice and so that they may fully accept those things which they acknowledge to be true, there is need for greater powers of speaking. Here entreaties and reproofs, exhortations and rebukes, and whatever other devices are necessary to move minds must be used.

7. And almost all men who make use of eloquence do not cease to do all of those things which I have mentioned.

V

But since some do these things dully, unevenly, and coldly, while others do them acutely, ornately, and vehemently, he should approach this work about which we are speaking who can dispute or speak wisely, even though he cannot do so eloquently, so that he may be of benefit to his hearers, even though he benefits them less than he would if he could also speak eloquently. But he who is foolish and abounds in eloquence is the more to be avoided the more he delights his auditor with those things to which it is useless to listen so that he thinks that because he hears a thing said eloquently it is true. This lesson, moreover, did not escape those who thought to teach the art of rhetoric. They granted that "wisdom without eloquence is of small benefit to states; but eloquence without wisdom is often extremely injurious and profits no one." [1] If those who taught the rules of eloquence, in the very books

[1] Cic. *De invent.* 1. 1. 1.

in which they did so, were forced by the power of truth to confess this, being ignorant of that true wisdom which descends supernal from the Father of Lights, how much more ought we, who are the sons and ministers of this wisdom, to think in no other way? For a man speaks more or less wisely to the extent that he has become more or less proficient in the Holy Scriptures. I do not speak of the man who has read widely and memorized much, but of the man who has well understood and has diligently sought out the sense of the Scriptures. For there are those who read them and neglect them, who read that they may remember but neglect them in that they fail to understand them. Those are undoubtedly to be preferred who remember the words less well, but who look into the heart of the Scriptures with the eye of their own hearts. But better than either of these is he who can quote them when he wishes and understands them properly.

8. For one who wishes to speak wisely, therefore, even though he cannot speak eloquently, it is above all necessary to remember the words of Scripture. The poorer he sees himself to be in his own speech, the more he should make use of Scripture so that what he says in his own words he may support with the words of Scripture. In this way he who is inferior in his own words may grow in a certain sense through the testimony of the great. He shall give delight with his proofs when he cannot give delight with his own words. Indeed, he who wishes to speak not only wisely but also eloquently, since he can be of more worth if he can do both, should more eagerly engage in reading or hearing the works of the eloquent and in imitating them in practice than in setting himself to learn from the masters of the art of rhetoric. But those to be read or heard should be those truly recommended not only for their eloquence but also for the fact that they have written or spoken wisely. For he who speaks eloquently is heard with pleasure; he who speaks wisely is heard with profit. Hence the Scripture does not say, "the multitude of the eloquent," but "the multitude of the wise is the welfare of the whole world." [2] Just as

2 Wisd. 6. 26.

things which are both bitter and healthful are frequently to be taken, so also a pernicious sweetness is always to be avoided. But what is better than a wholesome sweetness or a sweet wholesomeness? The more eagerly the sweetness is desired, the more readily the wholesomeness becomes profitable. There are men of the Church who treat the Scriptures not only wisely but eloquently. And there is not enough time for reading them, rather than that they could ever fail those who are studious and have leisure to read them.

VI

9. Here someone may inquire whether our authors, whose divinely inspired writings have formed the canon with a most wholesome authority for us, are merely wise or may also be called eloquent. This question is most easily solved for me and for those who think like me. For where I understand these authors, not only can nothing seem to me more wise than they are, but also nothing can seem more eloquent. And I venture to say that all who understand rightly what they say understand at the same time that it should not have been said in any other way. Just as there is a kind of eloquence for youth and another kind for age, that should not be called eloquence which is not appropriate to the person speaking. Thus there is a kind of eloquence fitting for men most worthy of the highest authority and clearly inspired by God. Our authors speak with eloquence of this kind, nor does any other kind become them. Nor is that kind suitable for others. It is suited to them, and the more it seems to fall below that of others, the more it exceeds them, not in pompousness but in solidity. Where I do not understand them, their eloquence appears to me to be less, but I do not doubt that it is like that eloquence I find in places where I do understand them. And the obscurity itself of the divine and wholesome writings was a part of a kind of eloquence through which our understandings should be benefited not only by the discovery of what lies hidden but also by exercise.

10. If there were time I could show all the virtues and ornaments of eloquence on account of which those are puffed up who place their own language above the language of our authors, not because of its greatness but because of its vanity, in those very sacred books which Divine Providence provided that we might be instructed and transferred from this evil world into a blessed world. But those things in that eloquence which our authors have in common with pagan orators and poets do not greatly delight me; I am more astonished and amazed that they have used our eloquence in such a way through another eloquence of their own that it seems neither lacking in them nor ostentatious in them. For it was not fitting for them either to condemn it or to make a display of it. The first might have been implied if they had avoided it, the second if they had too easily acknowledged it. And in those places where by chance eloquence is recognized by the learned, such things are said that the words with which they are said seem not to have been sought by the speaker but to have been joined to the things spoken about as if spontaneously, like wisdom coming from her house (that is, from the breast of the wise man) followed by eloquence as if she were an inseparable servant who was not called.

VII

11. Who would not see what the Apostle wished to say and how wisely he said it in the passage: "But we glory also in tribulations, knowing that tribulation worketh patience; and patience trial; and trial hope; and hope confoundeth not, because the charity of God is poured forth in our hearts, by the Holy Ghost, who is given to us"? [1] However, if anyone who is, if I may use the expression, unlearnedly learned, should contend that the Apostle followed the rules of the art of eloquence, would he not be ridiculed by both learned and unlearned Christians? And yet the figure which is called *klimax* in Greek and *gradatio* in Latin by some who do not wish to use the

[1] Rom. 5. 3-5.

word *scala* [ladder], where words or meanings are connected by proceeding one from the other, is recognizable in this passage. For we see that here patience arises from tribulation, trial from patience, and hope from trial. Another ornament is also apparent, for after certain locutions pronounced with the same expression, which our writers call *membra* and *caesa*, and the Greeks call *kola* and *kómmata*, there follows an *ambitus* or *circuitus*, which the Greeks call *periodos* [period], whose *membra* are held suspended by the voice of the speaker until the last one is completed. For of those *membra* preceding the *circuitus*, the first is "knowing that tribulation worketh patience," the second is "and patience trial," the third is "and trial hope." Then there follows the *circuitus* itself carried out in three *membra*, of which the first is "and hope confoundeth not," the second "because the charity of God is poured forth in our hearts," and the third "by the Holy Ghost, who is given to us." These and the like things are taught in the art of eloquence. But just as we do not say that the Apostle followed the precepts of eloquence, so also we do not deny that his wisdom was accompanied by eloquence.

12. Writing to the Corinthians in the second Epistle he refutes certain persons, pseudo-apostles from among the Jews, who had attacked him. And since he was forced to praise himself, attributing this praise to a kind of folly of his own, how wisely and how eloquently he speaks! Companion to wisdom and leader of eloquence, following the first and not scorning the second, he says: "I say again: let no man think me to be foolish, otherwise take me as one foolish, that I also may glory a little. That which I speak, I speak not according to God, but as it were in foolishness, in this matter of glorying. Seeing that many glory according to the flesh, I will glory also. For you gladly suffer the foolish, whereas yourselves are wise. For you suffer if a man bring you into bondage, if a man devour you, if a man take from you, if a man be lifted up, if a man strike you on the face. I speak according to dishonor, as if we had been weak in this part. Wherein if any man dare (I speak foolishly), I dare also. They are Hebrews? So am I. They are

Israelites? So am I. They are the seed of Abraham? So am I. They are the ministers of Christ? (I speak as one less wise) I am more; in many more labors, in prisons more frequently, in stripes above measure, in deaths often. Of the Jews five times did I receive forty stripes save one. Thrice was I beaten with rods, once I was stoned, thrice I suffered shipwreck, a night and a day I was in the depth of the sea. In journeying often, in perils of waters, in perils of robbers, in perils from my own nation, in perils from the Gentiles, in perils in the city, in perils in the wilderness, in perils in the sea, in perils from false brethren. In labor and painfulness, in much watchings, in hunger and thirst, in fastings often, in cold and nakedness. Besides those things which are without, my daily instance, the solicitude for all the churches. Who is weak, and I am not weak? Who is scandalized, and I am not on fire? If I must needs glory, I will glory of the things that concern my infirmity." [2] Those who are awake will see how much wisdom lies in these words. With what a river of eloquence they flow even he who snores must notice.

13. Moreover, the informed will recognize that those *caesa* which the Greeks call *kómmata*, and *membra* and *circuitus* which I mentioned a short time ago, since they are intermixed with a pleasing variety, make up the whole appearance of this passage, giving it, as it were, an outward expression by means of which even the unlearned are pleased. From the point at which we introduced the passage there are periods, the first of which is the least since it contains two *membra*, and a period may not have less than two *membra*, although it may have more. The first is then, "I say again: let no man think me to be foolish." This is followed by another of three *membra*, "otherwise, take me as one foolish, that I also may glory a little." The third which follows has four *membra*: "That which I speak, I speak not according to God, but as it were in foolishness, in this matter of glorying." The fourth has two: "Seeing that many glory according to the flesh, I will glory also." And the fifth has two: "For you gladly suffer the foolish,

2 2 Cor. 11. 16-30.

whereas yourselves are wise." Again, the sixth has two *membra:*
"For you suffer, if a man bring you into bondage." There follow three *caesa:* "if a man devour you, if a man take from
you, if a man be lifted up." Then there are three *membra:*
"if a man strike you on the face, I speak according to dishonor, as if we had been weak in this part." There is added a
circuitus or period of three *membra:* "Wherein if any man
dare (I speak foolishly), I dare also." Then three times *caesa*
are put as questions answered by three *caesa* used as answers:
"They are Hebrews? So am I. They are Israelites? So am I.
They are the seed of Abraham? So am I." The fourth of these
caesa is then put as a question and answered by a *membrum:*
"They are the ministers of Christ? (I speak as one less wise)
I am more." Then, the interrogatory form having been grace-
fully abandoned, the four following *caesa* are poured forth:
"in many more labors, in prisons frequently, in stripes above
measure, in deaths often." Then a brief *circuitus* is introduced,
since by the elevation of the voice "Of the Jews five times" is
to be distinguished so that it constitutes one *membrum* connected with the second, "did I receive forty stripes save one."
Then the voice returns to a series of *caesa,* of which there are
three: "Thrice was I beaten with rods, once I was stoned,
thrice I suffered shipwreck." There follows a *membrum:* "a
night and a day I was in the depths of the sea." Then fourteen
caesa are poured forth with a most pleasing vigor: "In journeying often, in perils of waters, in perils of robbers, in perils
from my own nation, in perils from the Gentiles, in perils in
the city, in perils in the wilderness, in perils in the sea, in
perils from false brethren, in labor and painfulness, in much
watchings, in hunger and thirst, in fastings often, in cold and
nakedness." After these there is a *circuitus* of three *membra:*
"Besides those things which are without, my daily instance, the
solicitude for all the churches." To these two *membra* are
joined as questions: "Who is weak, and I am not weak? Who
is scandalized, and I am not on fire?" Finally, this almost
breathless passage is ended with a *circuitus* of two *membra:*
"If I must needs glory, I will glory of the things that concern

my infirmity." After the force of this passage he rests as it were by including a little explanation, and he makes his hearer rest also with a charm and delight which I cannot sufficiently describe. For he continues, saying, "The God and Father of Our Lord Jesus Christ, who is blessed for ever, knoweth that I lie not." And then he tells very briefly how he was imperiled and how he escaped.

14. It would be tedious to present other instances or to show the same things in other passages of the Holy Scriptures. What if I had wished to point out the figures of speech taught in the art of rhetoric at least in those passages which I have quoted from the Apostle? Would not serious men have thought that I had said too much on the subject rather than enough to satisfy a student? When all these things are taught by masters, they are greatly esteemed, bought for a great price, and sold with boasting. I am ashamed to be tainted by this boasting when I discuss these things in this way. But ill-informed men are to be answered when they think to condemn our authors, not because they do not have, but because they do not show that eloquence which such men love too well.

15. But perhaps someone thinks that I have selected the Apostle Paul as our one eloquent speaker. When he says, "For although I be rude in speech, yet not in knowledge," [3] he seems to speak as though he were conceding to his critics rather than confessing something he recognized to be true. If, indeed, he had said, "I am rude in speech, but not in knowledge," he could not have been understood in any other way. He certainly did not hesitate to profess that knowledge without which he could not have been "a doctor of the Gentiles." [4] Surely, if we offer anything of his as an example of eloquence, we shall offer it from those Epistles which even his critics who wished to have his word seem contemptible confessed to be "weighty and strong." [5] It is therefore incumbent upon me to say something of the eloquence of the Prophets, where many things are obscured by tropes. The more these things seem to

[3] 2 Cor. 11. 6.   [5] 2 Cor. 10. 10.
[4] 1 Tim. 2. 7.

be obscured by figurative words, the sweeter they become when they are explained. But I should quote a passage where I am not forced to explain what is said but can devote my attention to commending the way in which it is said. And I may most readily do this by using the book of that prophet who said that he had been a shepherd or herdsman but had been sent by God away from his occupation to the end that he might prophesy God to the people.[6] But I shall not follow the Septuagint trans-lators, who, also inspired by the Holy Spirit, seem to have ex-pressed some things in a different way so that the labor of the reader might be directed to a scrutiny of the spiritual sense. Whence in that translation some things are more obscure, be-cause they are more figurative, than they are in the original. Rather I shall use these passages as they are translated by the priest, Jerome, a skilled translator who knew both languages.

16. When he was reproving the impious, the proud, the lecherous, and those therefore most neglectful of fraternal love, this rustic, or rustic turned prophet, exclaimed: "Woe to you that are wealthy in Sion, and to you that have confidence in the mountain of Samaria: ye great men, heads of the people, that go in with the state into the house of Israel. Pass ye over to Chalane, and see, and go from thence into Emath the great: and go down into Geth of the Philistines, and to all the best kingdoms of these: if their border be larger than your border. You that are separated unto the evil day: and that approach to the throne of iniquity; You that sleep upon beds of ivory, and are wanton on your couches: that eat the lambs out of the flock, and the calves out of the midst of the herd; You that sing to the sound of the psaltery: they have thought themselves to have instruments of music like David; That drink wine in bowls, and anoint themselves with the best ointments: and they are not concerned for the affliction of Joseph." [7] Would those who, considering themselves to be learned and eloquent, con-demn our Prophets as being unlearned and ignorant of elo-quence, have wished to speak otherwise if they had found it

[6] Amos 7. 14-15.   [7] Amos 6. 1-6.

necessary to say such things to such people, that is, those
among them who did not wish to rage?

17. For what more than this eloquence could sober ears desire? First of all, with what force is that invective hurled
against those who are as if asleep in their senses that they
may awaken! "Woe to you that are wealthy in Sion, and to
you that have confidence in the mountains of Samaria: ye great
men, heads of the people, that go in with the state into the
house of Israel." Then that he may show them ungrateful for
the benefits of God, who gave them ample space, in that they
have confidence in the mountains of Samaria where idols are
worshiped, he says: "Pass ye over to Chalane, and see, and go
from thence into Emath the great, and go down into Geth of
the Philistines, and to all the best kingdoms of these: if their
border be larger than your border." And while he is saying
these things, the names of places ornament his eloquence like
lights: Sion, Samaria, Chalane, Emath the Great, and Geth of
the Philistines. Then the words which join these places are
most effectively varied: "you that are wealthy, have confidence
in, pass ye over, go, go down."

18. Then he prophesies the approach of captivity under a
wicked king when he adds: "You that are separated unto the
evil day, and that approach to the throne of iniquity." Then
he adds because of lechery: "You that sleep upon beds of
ivory, and are wanton on your couches: that eat the lambs out
of the flock, and the calves out of the midst of the herd."
Those six *membra* formed three *circuitus* of two *membra*
each. For he does not say, "You that are separated unto the
evil day, you that approach to the throne of iniquity, you that
sleep upon beds of ivory, you that are wanton on your couches,
you that eat the lambs out of the flock, and the calves out of
the midst of the herd"; had he done so, the effect would have
been pleasant in that each of the six *membra* would depend
on the same pronoun repeated, and in pronunciation each
would have been terminated by the inflection of the voice. But
it is more beautiful as it stands in that two *membra* are joined
to each pronoun so that three sentences result. The first is a

prediction of captivity, "You that are separated unto the evil
day: and that approach to the throne of iniquity"; the second
pertains to lust, "You that sleep upon beds of ivory, and are
wanton on your couches"; the third pertains to gluttony,
"You that eat the lambs out of the flock, and the calves out
of the midst of the herd." In this way it is in the power of the
speaker to determine whether he shall close each *membrum*,
so that there are six, or whether he shall in speaking suspend
the first, third, and fifth, connecting the second to the first,
the fourth to the third, and the sixth to the fifth so that he
most effectively makes three *circuitus* of two *membra* each,
showing by the first the impending calamity, by the second the
impure bed, and by the third the groaning table.

19. Then he denounces the immoderate pleasure of the ears.
Here when he has said, "You that sing to the sound of the
psaltery," since music may be indulged wisely by the wise,
with a remarkable appropriateness of speech he relaxes the
impetus of his invective, and now speaking about them instead of to them so that we may be moved to distinguish between music among the wise and music among the lecherous,
he does not say, "You that sing to the sound of the psaltery,
you think yourselves to have instruments of music like David."
But when he has said to them what the lecherous should
hear, "You that sing to the sound of the psaltery," he in a certain way indicates their ignorance to others by adding, "they
have thought themselves to have instruments of music like
David, that drink wine in bowls and anoint themselves with
the best ointments." These three elements are best pronounced
if the first two *membra* of the *circuitus* are suspended and the
expression is completed by the third.

20. Now whether what is added to all of these things, "and
they are not concerned for the affliction of Joseph," is spoken
either continuously so as to make one *membrum* or it is better to suspend the voice after "they are not concerned" and to
add to it "for the affliction of Joseph" so as to make a *circuitus*
of two *membra*, it is with wonderful beauty that he did not
say "for the affliction of their brothers," but rather for their

brother "Joseph," so that any brother may be signified in the name of him whose fame is eminent among brothers, both because of the wrongs he suffered and because of the benefits he paid in return. I do not know whether this particular trope in accordance with which "Joseph" is made to stand for any brother is treated in that art which we learned and taught. But how beautiful it is, and how it affects those readers who understand it, it is useless to tell anyone who does not feel it himself.

21. And more things which pertain to the precepts of eloquence may be found in this same passage which we have used as an example. But a good listener warms to it not so much by diligently analyzing it as by pronouncing it energetically. For these words were not devised by human industry, but were poured forth from the divine mind both wisely and eloquently, not in such a way that wisdom was directed toward eloquence, but in such a way that eloquence did not abandon wisdom. If it is true, as some most learned and acute men were able to say, that those things which are taught in the art of oratory could not have been observed and noted and arranged systematically in that teaching unless they had been first found in the ingenuity of orators, what wonder is it that they are found in these men whom He sent who creates ingenuity? Therefore let us say that our canonical authors and teachers were not only wise but eloquent in that kind of eloquence which is appropriate for such persons.

VIII

22. Although we select certain examples of eloquence from their writings which may be understood without difficulty, nevertheless we should not think that we must imitate them in that which they have spoken with a useful and healthful obscurity for the purpose of exercising and sharpening, as it were, the minds of the readers and of destroying fastidiousness and stimulating the desire to learn, concealing their intention in such a way that the minds of the impious are either converted to piety or excluded from the mysteries of the faith.

Indeed, they spoke in this way so that those who understood and correctly explained them among their posterity might find a similar grace in the Church of God, not equal to theirs but at least approaching it. But their expositors should not for this reason so speak that they, having a similar authority, offer themselves for interpretation. But in all their utterances they should first of all seek to speak so that they may be understood, speaking in so far as they are able with such clarity that either he who does not understand is very slow or that the difficulty and subtlety lie not in the manner of speaking but in the things which we wish to explain and show, so that this is the reason why we are understood less, or more slowly.

IX

23. For there are some things which with their full implications are not understood or are hardly understood, no matter how eloquently they are spoken, or how often, or how plainly. And these things should never, or only rarely on account of some necessity, be set before a popular audience. In books, however—which, when they are understood, hold the readers to them in a certain way, and, when they are not understood, are not troublesome to those not wishing to read—and in conversations the duty should not be neglected of bringing the truth which we have perceived, no matter how difficult it may be to comprehend or how much labor may be involved, to the understanding of others, provided that the listener or disputant wishes to learn and has the capacity to do so no matter how the material is presented. The speaker should not consider the eloquence of his teaching but the clarity of it.

X

24. The desire of a person seeking such clarity sometimes neglects a more cultivated language, not caring for what sounds elegant but for what well indicates and suggests what he wishes to show. Hence a certain author who treats this kind of speaking says that there is in it "a kind of studied neg-

ligence." [1] This, however, takes away ornaments in such a way
that vulgarities do not result. But good teachers have, or
should have, such a desire to teach that if a word in good
Latin is necessarily ambiguous or obscure, the vulgar manner
of speech is used so that ambiguity or obscurity may be avoided
and the expression is not that of the learned but of the unlearned. For if our translators have not hesitated to say "I will
not gather together their meetings for blood offerings," [2] since
they thought it pertinent that this word [*sanguinibus*] be used
in the plural although it is used only in the singular in the
Latin language, why should a teacher of piety instructing the
unlearned hesitate to say *ossum* rather than *os* lest this syllable
be taken not as the singular of which *ossa* [bones] is the plural,
but as the singular of which *ora* [mouths] is the plural, since
African ears make no distinction between short and long
vowels? What profits correctness in a speech which is not followed by the listeners when there is no reason for speaking if
what is said is not understood by those on whose account we
speak? He who teaches should thus avoid all words which do
not teach. And if he can find other correct words which are
understood he should select those; but if he cannot find them,
either because they do not occur to him or because they do not
exist, he should use words less correct, provided that the thing
taught is taught and learned without distortion when they
are used.

25. This principle is valid not only in conversations whether
with one person or with several, but it is to be insisted upon
much more when sermons are delivered to the people so that
we may be understood. In a conversation anyone may ask questions. But where all are silent that one may be heard and all
are intent upon him, it is neither customary nor proper that
anyone inquire about what he does not understand. For this
reason the teacher should be especially careful to assist the
silent learner. However, an attentive crowd eager to comprehend usually shows by its motion whether it understands, and
until it signifies comprehension the matter being discussed

[1] Cic. *Orat.* 23. 77 ff.   [2] Ps. 15. 4 [16. 4].

should be considered and expressed in a variety of ways. But this technique may not be used by those who have prepared what they have to say and memorized it word for word. As soon as it is clear that the audience has understood, the discourse should be finished or another topic should be taken up. For just as a speaker who makes clear what is to be learned is pleasing, a speaker who insists on what is already known is burdensome, at least to those whose whole expectation depends on a solution of the difficulties in the matter being treated. However, for the sake of pleasing, things which are already known are also discussed where attention is given not to the things themselves but to the manner in which they are presented. And if this manner is already known and it still pleases the audience, it does not matter whether he who speaks is a speaker or a reader. For those things which are well written are not only read with pleasure by those becoming acquainted with them for the first time, but they are also reread not without pleasure by those who know them well and who have not forgotten them. And by both of these classes they are willingly heard. Moreover, that which a person has forgotten is taught to him when he is reminded of it. But I am not here treating the method of pleasing; I speak of the method of teaching those who wish to learn. And the best method is that in accordance with which he who hears, hears the truth, and understands what he hears. When this end is attained, nothing further is to be done with the matter as if to teach it more at length, but perhaps it should be commended so that it becomes fixed in the heart. If this seems the proper thing to do, it should be done moderately lest it lead to tedium.

XI

26. This eloquence is that to be used in teaching, not that the listener may be pleased by what has horrified him, nor that he may do what he has hesitated to do, but that he may be aware of that which lay hidden. However, if it is used unpleasantly, its fruits will come only to a few of the most stu-

dious who desire to learn what is to be taught no matter how
abjectly and rudely it is presented. And when they have obtained it, they feast delightedly on this truth, for it is a mark
of good and distinguished minds to love the truth within
words and not the words. Of what use is a gold key if it will
not open what we wish? Or what objection is there to a
wooden one which will, when we seek nothing except to open
what is closed? But since there is some comparison between
eating and learning, it may be noted that on account of the
fastidiousness of many even that food without which life is
impossible must be seasoned.

XII

27. Therefore a certain eloquent man said, and said truly,
that he who is eloquent should speak in such a way that he
teaches, delights, and moves. Then he added, "To teach is a
necessity, to please is a sweetness, to persuade is a victory." [1]
Of the three, that which is given first place, that is, the necessity of teaching, resides in the things which we have to say,
the other two in the manner in which we say it. Thus he who
speaks when he would teach cannot think that he has said what
he wished to say to the person he wishes to teach so long as
that person does not understand him. For even though he has
said something which he himself understands, he is not yet
to be thought of as having spoken to the person who does not
understand him; on the other hand, if he is understood, he
has spoken, no matter how he has spoken. But if he desires
also to delight or to move the person to whom he speaks he
will not do it simply by speaking in any way at all; but the
manner in which he speaks determines whether he does so.
Just as the listener is to be delighted if he is to be retained as
a listener, so also he is to be persuaded if he is to be moved
to act. And just as he is delighted if you speak sweetly, so is
he persuaded if he loves what you promise, fears what you
threaten, hates what you condemn, embraces what you com-

[1] Cic. *Orat.* 21. 69.

mend, sorrows at what you maintain to be sorrowful; rejoices when you announce something delightful, takes pity on those whom you place before him in speaking as being pitiful, flees those whom you, moving fear, warn are to be avoided; and is moved by whatever else may be done through grand eloquence toward moving the minds of listeners, not that they may know what is to be done, but that they may do what they already know should be done.

28. But if they still do not know this, instruction should come before persuasion. And perhaps when the necessary things are learned, they may be so moved by a knowledge of them that it is not necessary to move them further by greater powers of eloquence. But when it is necessary, it is to be done, and it is necessary when they know what should be done but do not do it. And for this reason teaching is a necessity. But men may act and still not act in accordance with what they know. But who would tell them to do something in accordance with what they do not know? And therefore persuasion is not a necessity because it need not always be applied if the listener consents through teaching and even through delight also. But it is also true that persuasion is victory, for people may be taught and pleased and still not consent. And of what use are the first two if the third does not follow? But delight is not a necessity either. Sometimes, when the truth is demonstrated in speaking, an action which pertains to the function of teaching, eloquence is neither brought into play nor is any attention paid to whether the matter or the discourse is pleasing, yet the matter itself is pleasing when it is revealed simply because it is true. Whence many are delighted simply by the exposure and refutation of falsehoods. These do not delight because they are falsehoods; but since it is true that they are false, the very language in which this is demonstrated to be true delights

XIII

29. Because of those whose fastidiousness is not pleased by truth if it is stated in any other way except in that way in

which the words are also pleasing, delight has no small place in the art of eloquence. But when this has been added it is not sufficient for the obdurate who have profited neither from understanding what was said nor from delighting in the manner in which it was taught. How do these help a man who both confesses the truth and praises the eloquence but still does not give his assent, on account of which alone the speaker, when he urges something, pays careful attention to the things which he is saying? When such things are taught that it is sufficient to know or to believe them, they require no more consent than an acknowledgment that they are true. But when that which is taught must be put into practice and is taught for that reason, the truth of what is said is acknowledged in vain and the eloquence of the discourse pleases in vain unless that which is learned is implemented in action. It is necessary therefore for the ecclesiastical orator, when he urges that something be done, not only to teach that he may instruct and to please that he may hold attention, but also to persuade that he may be victorious. For it now remains for that man, in whom the demonstration of truth, even when suavity of diction was added, did not move to consent, to be persuaded by the heights of eloquence.

XIV

30. So much care has been lavished on this suavity by men that writings are read which not only should not be put in practice but rather should be avoided and detested, since they contain only completely evil and wicked things urged by most vile and wicked men, not that they may win consent but only for the sake of pleasure. May God avert from His Church what the prophet Jeremias observed concerning the Synagogue of the Jews, saying: "Astonishing and wonderful things have been done in the land. The prophets prophesied falsehood, and the priests clapped their hands: and my people loved such

things: what then should be done in the end thereof?" [1] O
eloquence more terrible that it is more pure, and because it is
more genuine more powerful! Truly "a hammer that breaketh
the rock in pieces" ! [2] Through this very prophet God Himself
said that His word is like this hammer when it is spoken by
the holy Prophets. May it never happen, then. May it never
happen to us that our priests applaud those speaking iniquity
and that our people love such things! May this madness, I say,
never happen to us, for what should we do in the end? Let
those things which are said be said less clearly, less pleasingly,
less persuasively, but let them be said nevertheless; and may
the just rather than the wicked be willingly heard. But this
will not happen unless they speak pleasingly.

31. Among a strong people, concerning whom God says "I
will praise thee in a strong people," [3] that sweetness of discourse is not pleasing in which, although no iniquity is spoken,
trivial and fragile truths are ornamented with a frothy nexus
of words of a kind which could not properly be used to ornament even weighty and important matters. There is something
of this kind in an epistle of the blessed Cyprian which I think
either appeared accidentally or was deliberately included that
posterity might know that the sanity of Christian doctrine
restrained his tongue from these redundancies and restricted it
to a graver and more modest eloquence like that in the later
writings, which may be safely loved, religiously desired, but
imitated with difficulty. He says in one place, "Let us seek
this place; the neighboring solitudes offer a refuge where the
wandering tendrils of the vines twine through loaded trellises
with pendulous interlacings so as to make with a leafy roof
a woody colonnade." [4] This is not said without a remarkably
fluent fecundity of eloquence, but since it is burdened with
too much profusion it is displeasing. Those who admire this
sort of thing think that those who do not speak in this manner, but with more discipline, cannot do so, not realizing that

[1] Jer. 5. 30-31.   [3] Ps. 34. 18 [35. 18].
[2] Jer. 23. 29.   [4] Cypr. Ad Donat. 1.

they avoid the manner deliberately. On that account this holy man shows that he was able to speak in this way, since he did so once, but that he did not desire to do so, since he did not do so again.

XV

32. Thus this orator of ours, when he speaks of the just and holy and good—nor should he speak of anything else—so acts when he speaks that he may be understood and that he may be willingly and obediently heard. And he should not doubt that he is able to do these things, if he is at all able and to the extent that he is able, more through the piety of his prayers than through the skill of his oratory, so that, praying for himself and for those whom he is to address, he is a petitioner before he is a speaker. When the hour in which he is to speak approaches, before he begins to preach, he should raise his thirsty soul to God in order that he may give forth what he shall drink, or pour out what shall fill him. Since there are many things to be said concerning each thing to be treated according to faith and love, and many ways in which they may be said by those who know them, who knows better how we should say them or how they should be heard through us at the present time than He who sees "the hearts of all men"? [1] And who shall bring it about that we say what should be said through us and in the manner in which it should be said except Him, in whose "hand are both we, and our words"? [2] And for this reason, he who would both know and teach should learn everything which should be taught and acquire a skill in speaking appropriate to an ecclesiastic, but at the time of the speech itself he should think that which the Lord says more suitable to good thought: "Take no thought how or what to speak: for it shall be given you in that hour what to speak. For it is not you that speak, but the Spirit of your Father that speaketh in you." [3] If the Holy Spirit speaks in

1 Acts 1. 24.   3 Matt. 10. 19-20.
2 Wisd. 7. 16.

those who are given over to persecutors for the sake of Christ, why should it not also in those who give over Christ to learners?

XVI

33. If anyone says, however, that if teachers are made learned by the Holy Spirit they do not need to be taught by men what they should say or how they should say it, he should also say that we should not pray because the Lord says, "for your Father knoweth what is needful for you, before you ask him," [1] or that the Apostle Paul should not have taught Timothy and Titus what or how they should teach others. A man upon whom is imposed the person of a teacher in the Church should have these three Apostolic Epistles before his eyes. Do we not read in the first Epistle to Timothy, "These things command and teach"? [2] What these things are is explained previously. Do not we find there, "An ancient man rebuke not, but treat him as a father"? [3] And in the second Epistle is it not said, "Hold the form of sound words, which thou hast heard of me"? [4] And is it not there said to him, "Carefully study to present thyself approved unto God, a workman that needeth not to be ashamed, rightly handling the word of truth"? [5] There also we find this: "Preach the word: be instant in season, out of season: reprove, entreat, rebuke in all patience and doctrine." [6] Again, does he not say to Titus that a bishop should persevere in "that faithful word which is according to doctrine, that he may be able to exhort in sound doctrine, and to convince the gainsayers"? [7] There he also says, "But speak thou the things that become sound doctrine: that the aged men be sober," [8] and so on. And this too: "These things speak, and exhort and rebuke with all authority. Let no man despise thee. Admonish them to be

[1] Matt. 6. 8.
[2] 1 Tim. 4. 11.
[3] 1 Tim. 5. 1.
[4] 2 Tim. 1. 13.
[5] 2 Tim. 2. 15.
[6] 2 Tim. 4. 2.
[7] Titus 1. 9.
[8] Titus 2. 1-2.

subject to princes and powers," etc.[9] What are we to think? Does the Apostle contradict himself when he says that men are made teachers by the operation of the Holy Spirit and at the same time tells them what and how they should teach? Or is it to be understood that the office of men in teaching even these teachers should not cease even with the generosity of the Holy Spirit assisting? For "neither he that planteth is anything, nor he that watereth; but God that giveth the increase." [10] Whence it happens that even with the assistance of holy men, or even if the holy angels themselves take part, no one rightly learns those things which pertain to life with God unless he is made by God docile to God, to whom it is said in the Psalm, "teach me to do thy will, for thou art my God." [11] Whence also the Apostle says to that same Timothy, speaking as a teacher to his disciple, "But continue thou in those things which thou hast learned, and which have been committed to thee, knowing of whom thou hast learned them." [12] Medicines for the body which are administered to men by men do not help them unless health is conferred by God, who can cure without them; yet they are nevertheless applied even though they are useless without His aid. And if they are applied courteously, they are considered to be among works of mercy or kindness. In the same way, the benefits of teaching profit the mind when they are applied by men, when assistance is granted by God, who could have given the gospel to man even though it came not from men nor through a man.[13]

XVII

34. He who seeks to teach in speech what is good, spurning none of these three things, that is, to teach, to delight, and to persuade, should pray and strive that he be heard intelligently, willingly, and obediently. When he does this well and properly, he can justly be called eloquent, even though he

---

9 Titus 2. 15-3. 1.   12 2 Tim. 3. 14.
10 1 Cor. 3. 7.   13 Cf. Gal. 1. 1.
11 Ps. 142. 10 [143. 10].

fails to win the assent of his audience. To these three things—
that he should teach, delight, and persuade—the author of
Roman eloquence himself seems to have wished to relate three
other things when he said, "He therefore will be eloquent who
can speak of small things in a subdued manner, of moderate
things in a temperate manner, and of grand things in a grand
manner." [1] It is as though he had added these to the three
mentioned previously and said, "He is therefore eloquent who
in order to teach, can speak of small things in a subdued
manner, and in order to please, can speak of moderate things
in a temperate manner, and in order to persuade, can speak
of great things in a grand manner."

XVIII

35. He could have demonstrated these three things as he
explains them in legal cases, but he could not have done so in
ecclesiastical questions of the kind with which the speech
which we wish to cultivate will be called upon to concern
itself. In legal questions those things are called "small" which
are concerned in cases involving money; they are called
"great" when they have to do with human welfare or life.
Those cases in which neither of these is to be judged and
nothing is advanced to make the listener judge or act, but
what is said is set forth only to please him, the matter is said
to be as if in between and on this account called middling or
"moderate." "Moderate" comes from *modus,* "measure," so
that we do not speak properly when we use "moderate" pejora-
tively to mean "small." Among our orators, however, everything we say, especially when we speak to the people from the
pulpit, must be referred, not to the temporal welfare of man,
but to his eternal welfare and to the avoidance of eternal
punishment, so that everything we say is of great importance,
even to the extent that pecuniary matters, whether they concern loss or gain, or large or small amounts of money, should

[1] Cic. *Orat.* 29. 101. *Submissus* is here translated "subdued" rather than
"plain" or "simple," both of which would be misleading in this context.

not be considered "small" when they are discussed by the Christian teacher. For neither is justice small, since we ought to maintain it even with reference to small amounts of money, for, as the Lord says, "He that is faithful in that which is least, is faithful also in that which is greater."[1] Therefore, what is least is least, but to be faithful in what is least is great. Just as in the nature of a circle all lines drawn from the center to the circumference are equal, and the same holds true whether we are examining a large disc or a very small coin, in the same way when justice is applied to small things justice itself is not diminished.

36. When the Apostle spoke of worldly cases (and which of them is not concerned with money?) he said: "Dare any of you, having a matter against another, go to be judged before the unjust, and not before the saints? Know you not that the saints shall judge this world? And if the world shall be judged by you, are you unworthy to judge the smallest matters? Know you not that we shall judge angels? How much more things of this world! If therefore you have judgments of things pertaining to this world, set them to judge, who are the most despised in the church. I speak to your shame. Is it so that there is not among you any one wise man, that is able to judge between his brethren? But brother goeth to law with brother, and that before unbelievers. Already indeed there is plainly a fault among you, that you have lawsuits one with another. Why do you not rather take wrong? Why do you not rather suffer yourselves to be defrauded? But you do wrong and defraud, and that to your brethren. Know you not that the unjust shall not possess the kingdom of God?"[2] What so angers the Apostle that he upbraids, reproves, reproaches, and threatens in this way? Why is it that he shows his emotion with such repeated bitter expressions? Finally, why does he speak of such small things in such a grand manner? Did that worldly business merit it? Not at all. He did this on account of justice, charity, piety, which, as no sober mind will doubt, are great even in the smallest things.

[1] Luke 16. 10.   [2] 1 Cor. 6. 1-9.

37. Certainly, if we were advising men how they should act in worldly cases, either for themselves or for their friends, before ecclesiastical judges, we should rightly urge them to speak in a subdued manner as if of small things. But when we are speaking of the eloquence of those men whom we wish to be teachers of things which will liberate us from eternal evil or lead us to eternal good, wherever these things are discussed, either before the people or in private, either with one or with several, either with friends or with enemies, either in extended speech or in conversation, either in treatises or in books, either in long letters or in short, they are great things. Unless, perhaps, because a cup of cold water is a small and most insignificant thing, we should also regard as small and most insignificant the promise of the Lord that he who gives such a cup to one of His disciples "shall not lose his reward." [3] Or when our teacher in the Church makes a sermon on this text, he should feel that he is speaking about a small thing so that he should speak, not in a moderate manner and not in a grand manner, but in a subdued manner. When we happen to speak about this matter before the people, and God assists so that we do not speak ineptly, does not a certain flame rise up as if from that cold water [4] which even inflames the cold breasts of men to perform acts of mercy in the hope of heavenly reward?

XIX

38. Nevertheless, although our teacher should speak of great things, he should not always speak about them in the grand manner, but in a subdued manner when he teaches something, in a moderate manner when he condemns or praises something. But when something is to be done and he is speaking to those who ought to do it but do not wish to do it, then those great things should be spoken in the grand manner in a way appropriate to the persuasion of their minds. And sometimes concerning one and the same important thing, he speaks in a subdued manner if he teaches, in a moderate manner if

---

[3] Matt. 10. 42.   [4] Cf. 2 Mach. [2 Macc.] 1. 32.

he is praising it, and in a grand manner if he is moving an adverse mind to conversion. For what is greater than God? Should nothing then be learned about Him? Or should he who teaches the unity of the Trinity use nothing except the subdued style so that he may make a thing very difficult to understand comprehensible in so far as is possible? Or should ornaments and not proofs be sought here? Or is the listener to be persuaded to do something and not rather instructed that he may learn? Again, when God is praised either on His own account or because of His works, what an appearance of beautiful and splendid diction arises in him who praises Him as he is able, whom no one praises adequately and whom no one in one way or another fails to praise! And if He is not worshiped, or if idols are worshiped with Him or before Him, or demons, or creatures of any kind, the orator should speak in a grand style of how great that evil is so that men may be averted from it.

XX

39. That what I say may be more plain, here is an example from the Apostle Paul of the subdued style: "Tell me, you that desire to be under the law, have you not read the law? For it is written that Abraham had two sons: the one by a bondwoman, and the other by a freewoman. But he who was of the bondwoman, was born according to the flesh: but he of the freewoman was by promise. Which things are said by an allegory. For these are the two testaments: the one from mount Sina, engendering unto bondage, which is Agar: For Sina is a mountain in Arabia, which hath affinity to that Jerusalem which now is, and is in bondage with her children. But that Jerusalem which is above, is free: which is our mother." [1] Again, where he reasons, and says; "Brethren (I speak after the manner of man) yet a man's testament, if it be confirmed, no man despiseth, nor addeth to it. To Abraham were the promises made and to his seed. He saith not, 'And to his seeds,'

[1] Gal. 4. 21-26.

as of many: but as of one, 'And to thy seed,' which is Christ. Now this I say, that the testament which was confirmed by God, the law which was made after four hundred and thirty years, doth not disannul, to make the promise of no effect. For if the inheritance be of the law, it is no more of promise. But God gave it to Abraham by promise." [2] And since it might occur to the mind of the listener to ask, "Why, then, was the Law given, if there is no inheritance from it?", he introduces this himself and says as if asking, "Why then was the law?" Then he answers, "It was set because of transgressions, until the seed should come, to whom he made the promise, being ordained by angels in the hand of a mediator. Now a mediator is not of one: but God is one." And here occurs an objection which he himself proposed, "Was the law then against the promises of God?" And he answers, "God forbid." And he gives a reason, saying, "For if there had been a law given which could give life, verily justice should have been by the law. But the scripture hath included all under sin, that the promise, by the faith of Jesus Christ, might be given to them that believe," etc.[3] Or similar examples could be cited. It is relevant to teaching not only to explain those things that are hidden and to solve the difficulties of questions, but also, while these things are being done, to introduce other questions which might by chance occur, lest what is said be rendered improbable or be refuted by them. But they should be introduced in such a way that they are answered at the same time, lest we introduce something we cannot remove. However, it sometimes happens that when questions contingent upon the main question, and still other questions contingent upon these, are introduced and solved, the process of reasoning is extended to such a length that the disputant, unless he has a very strong and vigorous memory, cannot return to the original topic. Nevertheless, it is good practice to refute such objections as may occur, lest one appear where there is no one to refute it, or lest it occur to someone who is present but is silent about it so that he goes away with less benefit.

[2] Gal. 3. 15-18. [3] Gal. 3. 19-22.

40. In the following words of the Apostle the style is moderate: "An ancient man rebuke not, but treat him as a father: young men, as brethren: Old women, as mothers: young women, as sisters." [4] And in these: "I beseech you, therefore, brethren, by the mercy of God, that you present your bodies a living sacrifice, holy, pleasing unto God." [5] And almost all the exhortation in this place shows the moderate style of eloquence. But it is more beautiful in those places where related things proceed from each other, as if those things which should be done were done: "And having different gifts, according to the grace that is given us, either prophecy, to be used according to the rule of faith; Or ministry, in ministering; or he that teacheth, in doctrine; He that exhorteth, in exhorting; he that giveth, with simplicity; he that ruleth, with carefulness; he that sheweth mercy, with cheerfulness. Let love be without dissimulation. Hating that which is evil, cleaving to that which is good: Loving one another with the charity of brotherhood, with honour preventing one another, In carefulness not slothful, in spirit fervent, serving the Lord, Rejoicing in hope, patient in tribulation, instant in prayer, Communicating to the necessities of the saints, pursuing hospitality. Bless them that persecute you: bless, and curse not. Rejoice with them that rejoice; weep with them that weep. Being of one mind one towards another." And when these things have been poured forth, how beautifully they are brought to a close with a *circuitus* of two *membra:* "not minding high things, but consenting to the humble"! [6] He says a little further on: "serving unto this purpose, render therefore to all men their dues: tribute, to whom tribute is due: custom, to whom custom: fear, to whom fear: honour, to whom honour." And when these *membra* have been spoken, they are closed again with a *circuitus* of two *membra:* "Owe no man anything, but to love one another." [7] And a little later on he says, "The night is passed, and the day is at hand. Let us therefore cast off the works of darkness, and put on the

4 1 Tim. 5. 1-2.   6 Rom. 12. 6-16.
5 Rom. 12. 1.   7 Rom. 13. 6-8.

armour of light. Let us walk honestly as in the day, not in rioting and drunkenness, not in chambering and impurities, not in contention and envy: But put ye on the Lord Jesus Christ, and make not provision for the flesh in its concupiscences." [8] If someone were to arrange this last clause *Et carnis providentiam ne in concupiscentiis feceritis* [instead of *et carnis providentiam ne feceritis in concupiscentiis*], it would undoubtedly please the ear with a more rhythmic close,[9] but the graver translator has preferred to keep the original word order. How this sounds in Greek pronunciation, as the Apostle spoke it, those who are learned in this language even to this point may decide. To me it seems that the word order, the same as that of our translation, does not run rhythmically there either.

41. It must be admitted that our authors are lacking in that rhetorical ornament which consists of rhythmic closings. Whether this situation was brought about by the translators or whether (as I think plausible) they themselves avoided such obvious devices, I cannot say, since I confess I do not know. This, however, I do know, that if someone skilled in this kind of rhythm would arrange their endings in accordance with the law of such rhythms, a feat which could easily be accomplished either by substituting certain words which have the same meaning or by changing the order of the words already there, he would recognize that not one of those things which are so highly regarded and taught in the schools of grammarians or rhetoricians is lacking in the writings of these holy men. And he will find many kinds of expression of such beauty that they are beautiful in our language, although especially beautiful in theirs, which are not found at all in that literature concerning which they are so vain. But caution must be exercised lest, when rhythm is added to the divine writings, their gravity be impaired. However, the musical discipline where rhythm [i.e., number] is fully learned, is not lacking in our Prophets, for

8 Rom. 13. 12-14.
9 On rhythmic closes, see H. I. Marrou, *Saint Augustin et la fin de la culture antique* (Paris, 1938), pp. 80-81.

the most learned Jerome observes meter in some of them as
they exist in the Hebrew tongue, although he has not translated them metrically because he wished to keep the verbal
accuracy of his translation. However, to speak of my own
opinion, which I know better than that of others and better
than others know it, although in my own expression I do not
neglect these rhythmical endings altogether in so far as they
may be used moderately, it pleases me more to find them very
rarely in the writings of our authors.

42. The grand style differs from the moderate style not so
much in that it is adorned with verbal ornaments but in that
it is forceful with emotions of the spirit. Although it uses
almost all of the ornaments, it does not seek them if it does
not need them. It is carried along by its own impetus, and if
the beauties of eloquence occur they are caught up by the
force of the things discussed and not deliberately assumed for
decoration. It is enough for the matter being discussed that
the appropriateness of the words be determined by the ardor
of the heart rather than by careful choice. For if a strong man
is armed with a gilded and bejeweled sword, and he is fully
intent on the battle, he does what he must with the arms he
has, not because they are precious but because they are arms.
Yet he is himself the same, and very powerful, even when
"wrath provides a weapon as he seeks one." [10] The Apostle
urges that the evils of this world are to be suffered for the sake
of the evangelical ministry, since all things may be tolerated
with the solace of God's gifts. It is a great subject, and it is
grandly presented, nor are the ornaments of speech lacking:
"Behold," he says, "now is the acceptable time; behold, now is
the day of salvation. Giving no offense to any man, that our
ministry be not blamed: But in all things let us exhibit ourselves as the ministers of God, in much patience, in tribulation,
in necessities, in distresses, In stripes, in prisons, in seditions,
in labours, in watchings, in fastings, In chastity, in knowledge,
in long-suffering, in sweetness, in the Holy Ghost, in charity
unfeigned, In the word of truth, in the power of God; by the

[10] Cf. Virg. *Aen.* 7. 507.

armour of justice on the right hand and on the left; Through
honour and dishonour, through evil report and good report;
as deceivers, and yet true; as unknown, and yet known; As
dying, and behold we live; as chastised, and not killed; As
sorrowful, yet always rejoicing; as needy, yet enriching many;
as having nothing, and possessing all things." Behold him still
fervent: "Our mouth is open to you, O ye Corinthians, our
heart is enlarged," and so on, but it would take too long to
follow it all.[11]

43. Again, he urges the Romans to conquer the persecutions
of this world by charity, with a sure hope in the help of God.
He speaks both grandly and ornately: "And we know that to
them that love God, all things work together unto good, to
such as, according to his purpose, are called to be saints. For
whom he foreknew, he also predestinated to be made conformable to the image of his Son; that he might be the firstborn
amongst many brethren. And whom he predestinated, them he
also called. And whom he called, them he also justified. And
whom he justified, them he also glorified. What shall we say
then to these things? If God be for us, who is against us? He
that spared not even his own Son, but delivered him up for us
all, how hath he not also, with him, given us all things! Who
shall accuse against the elect of God? God that justifieth? Who
is he that shall condemn? Christ Jesus that died, yea that is
risen also again; who is at the right hand of God, who also
maketh intercession for us? Who then shall separate us from
the love of Christ? Shall tribulation? or distress? or famine? or
nakedness? or danger? or persecution? or the sword? As it is
written: For thy sake we are put to death all the day long. We
are accounted as sheep for the slaughter. But in all these
things we overcome, because of him that hath loved us. For I
am sure that neither death, nor life, nor angels, nor principali-
ties, nor powers, nor things present, nor things to come, nor
might, nor height, nor depth, nor any other creature shall be
able to separate us from the love of God, which is in Christ
Jesus our Lord." [12]

[11] 2 Cor. 6. 2-11.   [12] Rom. 8. 28-39.

44. Although almost all of the Epistle to the Galatians is written in the subdued style, except the beginning and the end, which are in the moderate style, nevertheless he inserts one passage with such emotion that, without any ornaments like those in the passages quoted as examples heretofore, it cannot be spoken except in the grand style. "You observe," he says, "days, and months, and times, and years. I am afraid of you, lest perhaps I have laboured in vain among you. Be ye as I, because I also am as you: brethren, I beseech you. You have not injured me at all. And you know how through infirmity of the flesh, I preached the gospel to you heretofore: and your temptation in my flesh, You despised not, nor rejected, but received me as an angel of God, even as Christ Jesus. Where is then your blessedness? For I bear you witness, that if it could be done, you would have plucked out your own eyes, and would have given them to me. Am I then become your enemy, because I tell you the truth? They are zealous in your regard not well: but they would exclude you, that you might be zealous for them. But be zealous for that which is good in a good thing always: and not only when I am present with you. My little children, of whom I am in labour again, until Christ be formed in you. And I would willingly be present with you now, and change my voice: because I am ashamed for you." [13] Are contrary words set against their contraries here, or are things arranged climactically, or are *caesa* and *membra* and *circuitus* used? Yet not on that account is the grand emotion which we feel in the fervor of this eloquence diminished.

XXI

45. Although these apostolic words are clear, they are also profound, and they are so written and commended to posterity that not only the reader or hearer but even the expositor has a task to perform if he is not content with their surfaces and seeks their depths. On this account, let us examine these styles of speaking in those who by reading the Scriptures became

[13] Gal. 4. 10-20.

proficient in the knowledge of divine and salutary truths and are at the same time ministers of the Church. The blessed Cyprian uses the subdued style in that book where he discusses the sacrament of the chalice. There he resolves the question as to whether or not the Lord's chalice should contain water alone or water mixed with wine. By way of example, something from this discussion may be used. After the beginning of his epistle, he sets out to resolve the question: "You know that we have been admonished to follow the Lord's example in offering the chalice, and that nothing should be done by us other than that which the Lord first did for us, so that the chalice which is offered in His commemoration should contain water mixed with wine. For since Christ says, 'I am the true vine,' [1] the blood of Christ is not water at all but wine. Nor can it be held that His blood, by which we are redeemed and vivified, is in the chalice when it contains no wine, through which the blood of Christ is shown, as is foretold by all the mysteries and testimonies of the Scriptures. Thus we find in Genesis concerning the sacrament that Noah prefigured it, and presented a figure of the Lord's Passion in that he drank wine, that he became inebriated, that he was naked in his house, that he lay naked with his limbs and thighs exposed, that the nakedness of the father was pointed out by his second son but covered by the oldest and youngest, and that other things happened which it is not necessary to refer to here, since it is enough to understand that when Noah showed the type of truth to come, he drank not water but wine, and so expressed the image of the Lord's Passion. Again, we see the Lord's sacrament prefigured in the priest Melchisedech, according to what the holy Scripture testifies, saying, 'But Melchisedech the king of Salem, bringing forth bread and wine, for he was the priest of the most high God, blessed [Abraham].' [2] The Holy Spirit declares in the Psalms that Melchisedech bore the type of Christ, saying in the person of the Father to the Son, 'Thou art a priest forever according to the order of Melchisedech.' " [3]

1 John 15. 1.   3 Ps. 109. 4 [110. 4].
2 Gen. 14. 18-19.

These and the other things which follow in this epistle [4] are in the manner of the subdued style, as the reader may easily discover.

46. St. Ambrose also, when he is urging a very important matter concerning the Holy Spirit, so that he may show it to be equal with the Father and the Son, nevertheless uses the subdued manner of speaking. For the thing discussed does not need verbal ornaments, nor motions of the affections to persuade, but evidence as proof. Thus among other things at the beginning of this work he says, "Gedeon was disturbed by the divine message when he heard that, although thousands of people were failing, the Lord would free his people from their enemies through one man. He offered the kid of goats and placed its flesh together with unleavened loaves on the rock in accordance with the precept of the Angel, and poured the broth on them. When the Angel touched these things together with the tip of the rod he was carrying, fire arose from the rock so that the sacrifice which was offered was consumed.[5] This evidence seems to show that the rock bore the type of the Body of Christ, for it is written, 'and they drank of the spiritual rock that followed them, and the rock was Christ.' [6] This clearly refers not to His divinity but to His flesh, which has flooded the thirsty hearts of the people with the unfailing stream of His blood. Then it was also announced in this mystery that Lord Jesus in the crucifixion of His flesh should abolish not only crimes committed but also the lusts of the heart. For the flesh of the kid refers to the guilt of actions, the broth to the evils of concupiscence, as in the passage, 'For . . . a multitude of people . . . burned with desire . . . and said, Who will give us flesh to eat?' [7] That the angel extended the rod and touched the rock from which fire came forth shows that the flesh of the Lord, filled with the Holy Spirit, would burn away all the sins of the human condition. Whence the Lord Himself says, 'I am come to cast fire on the earth.' " [8]

[4] Cypr. Epist. 63 ad Caecilium.   [7] Num. 11. 4.
[5] Judg. 6. 11-21.   [8] Luke 12. 49.
[6] 1 Cor. 10. 4.

The passage continues, in which he is concerned with teaching and offering proof.[9]

47. This praise of virginity from Cyprian is in the moderate style: "Now we address ourselves to virgins, who because of their greater glory deserve our greater care. They are the flower of the seed of the Church, the beauty and ornament of spiritual grace, the joyful inward nature of praise and honor, a whole and uncorrupted work, an image of God reflecting the sanctity of the Lord, the more illustrious part of the flock of Christ. The glorious fruitfulness of Mother Church rejoices in them and in them profusely flowers. The more glorious virginity adds to her number, the more the joy of the Mother increases." And in another place at the end of the epistle, he says, " 'As we have borne the image of the earthly, let us bear also the image of the heavenly.' [10] This image virginity bears; integrity bears it; sanctity and truth bear it. Those mindful of the discipline of God bear it, maintaining justice with religion, stable in faith, humble in fear, strong to bear all, meek to sustain injuries, eager to perform works of mercy, united and harmonious in fraternal peace. Each of these, O good virgins, you should observe, love, and fulfill your duties, you who, devoting yourselves to God and to Christ, should lead the way, being in a greater and better status, to the Lord to whom you have dedicated yourselves. You who are advanced in years should teach the younger; you who are younger, assist the ministry of the older and be an incitement to your peers; inspire one another with mutual encouragement; urge one another to glory by examples of virtue; persevere strongly, go forward spiritually, and attain your end happily; remember us when virginity begins to be honored in you." [11]

48. Ambrose also in a moderate but ornamented style sets forth to religious virgins, as it were in an example, what they should imitate in their manners. He says, "She was a virgin not only in body but also in mind. Her sincere disposition was not stained by any traces of deceit. She was humble in heart,

[9] Ambrose, *De Spir. sancto*, Prol.   [11] Cypr. *De hab. virg.* 3. 23.
[10] 1 Cor. 15. 49.

grave in discourse, prudent in mind, sparing in speech, studious in learning. She placed her hope, not in the uncertainty
of wealth, but in the prayer of the poor man. She was attentive
to her work, shamefast in speech. She customarily sought not
man but God as the guide to her mind. She injured no one,
but had good will toward all; she assented to her elders, and
did not envy her equals; she fled boasting, followed reason,
loved virtue. When did this one injure her parents, even with
a glance? When did she quarrel with her relatives? When did
she disdain the humble? When did she deride the weak? When
did she avoid the needy? She was accustomed to visit only
those gatherings of men at which mercy would not be ashamed
nor shame terrified. There was no arrogance in her eyes, no
boldness in her voice, no shamelessness in her actions. Her
bearing was not too faint, her gait not too loose, her voice not
too sensual, so that the very appearance of her body was an
image of her mind and a figure of probity. Certainly a good
house should be recognizable at its threshold, and should
show at the very entrance that no darkness lies within, as if the
light of the lamp inside illuminates the exterior. Why should
I describe her sparingness with food, her insistent kindness,
the one excessive beyond nature, the other almost less than
nature itself? In the one there was no intermission of time, in
the other days of fasting were doubled; and when the desire
to eat appeared, the food offered was often only of such a
character as to prevent death, not to minister to delights," etc.
I have offered this as an example of the moderate style, since
he is not here urging that anyone take vows of virginity who
has not already done so, but simply explaining how those who
have already taken such vows should act.[12] For in order that
the mind may be moved toward a proposal of such importance,
it must be excited and inflamed by the grand style. But the
martyr Cyprian wrote concerning the habit of virgins and not
of taking vows of virginity. However, this bishop arouses them
with great eloquence even to this.

49. But I shall now offer examples of the grand manner of

[12] Ambr. *De virg.* 2. 1. 7-8.

speaking concerning a subject which both men have discussed. Both men have condemned those women who color, or discolor, their features with paint. When the first discusses this matter, he says, among other things, "If an artist had depicted the face and form of a man and indicated the quality of his body with colors rivaling those of the original, and when the likeness was complete and finished another set his hand to it, as if being more skillful he would reshape the picture already made, this would be seen as a grave injury to the first artist and a reason for just indignation. Do you think that you can with impunity commit such a rash and wrongful act offensive to God the artist? Even though you may not be shameless concerning men nor defiled in mind by alluring rouges, you make yourself worse than an adulteress by corrupting and defiling those things which are God's. What you think ornaments you, what you think makes you more beautiful, is an attack on the divine work, a corruption of the truth. The voice of the Apostle warns: 'Purge out the old leaven, that you may be a new paste, as you are unleavened. For Christ our pasch is sacrificed. Therefore let us feast, not with the old leaven, nor with the leaven of malice and wickedness; but with the unleavened bread of sincerity and truth.' [13] Are sincerity and truth preserved when those things which are sincere are polluted and truth is changed into falsehood by adulterating colors and the tricks of cosmetics? Your Lord says, 'Thou canst not make one hair white or black'; [14] and you, in order to refute the word of your Lord, wish to be stronger. With brazen audacity and sacrilegious contempt you dye your hair; as an evil omen of the future, your hair already presages flames." [15] It would take too long to insert all that follows.

50. Ambrose discusses such things. "From these things," he says, "proceed incentives to vices in that they paint their faces with artificial colors when they are afraid to displease men, and the adulterated face implies an adulteration of chastity. What a piece of foolishness is this, to change the image of

[13] 1 Cor. 5. 7-8.   [15] Cypr. *De hab. virg.* 15 f.
[14] Matt. 5. 36.

nature and to seek a picture, and in dreading the adverse judgment of their husbands on their faces to reveal their own! For she passes a judgment on herself who desires to change that which is natural to her; thus when she seeks to please others she reveals her own prior displeasure. What more veracious judge do we need, woman, than yourself, when you are afraid to be seen? If you are beautiful, why do you hide? If you are ugly, why do you lie in implying that you are beautiful, since you will have neither the reward of your own conscience nor that of another's deception? If he loves another, you wish to please another; and you are angry if he loves another and was taught by you to be adulterous. You are the bad teacher of your own injury. For even she who has suffered from it flees from the art of the pander, and although she is a wicked woman, she sins not against another but against herself. Crimes of adultery are almost more endurable, for there shame is corrupted while here nature is adulterated." [16] It is sufficiently apparent, I think, that women are vehemently urged by this eloquence not to adulterate their appearance with rouge and to be shameful and fearful. Thus we recognize that the style is neither subdued nor moderate, but altogether grand. And in these two whom from among all writers I chose to quote, and in many writings of other ecclesiastical authors who say good things and say them well, that is, as the matter demands, acutely, ornately, or ardently, these three styles may be found. And students may learn them by assiduous reading, or hearing, accompanied by practice.

XXII

51. But no one should think that it is contrary to theory to mix these three manners; rather, speech should be varied with all types of style in so far as this may be done appropriately. For when one style is maintained too long, it loses the listener. When transitions are made from one to another, even though the speech is long, it proceeds more effectively, although each

[16] Ambr. *De virg.* 1. 6. 28.

style has its own varieties in the discourse of eloquent men by means of which the senses of the audience are not permitted to cool or languish. However, the subdued style alone can be tolerated more readily for a period of time than the grand style alone. Indeed, the more the mind of the listener is aroused so that he may agree with us, the less time it can be maintained in that state, once it has been sufficiently aroused. Thus we must be cautious lest when we wish to arouse what is already aroused, it may fall from that height to which it was brought by our stimulating it. When those things which must be said in the subdued style have been interposed, we return effectively to those things which must be said in the grand style, so that the impetus of our speech ebbs and flows like the sea. Whence it is true that if the grand style must be used for a protracted time, it should not be used alone, but should be varied by the intermingling of other styles. But the whole speech is said to be in that style which is used most in it so that it predominates.

XXIII

52. It is important to consider what style should be used to vary what other style, and what style should be employed in specific places. Thus even in the grand style the beginning of the discourse should always, or almost always, be moderate. And it is within the power of the speaker that he say some things in the subdued style which might be spoken in the grand style so that those things which are spoken in the grand style may seem more grand by comparison and be rendered more luminous as if by shadows. But in whatever style the difficulties of questions are to be solved, there is need for acumen, which the subdued style appropriates to itself. Thus this style is to be used with either of the other two when such matters appear in them. In the same way when praise or blame is a part of the matter, and neither the condemnation nor the liberation of anyone, nor assent to any other action is being urged, the moderate style should be employed, no matter which of the other two is being used. Therefore in the grand

style the two others have a place, and the same is true of the subdued style. The temperate style sometimes but not always needs the subdued style if, as I have said, a question arises to be solved, or, when some things which could be expressed with ornament are left plain and spoken in the subdued manner so that certain extravagances, so to speak, of ornament may seem more eminent. But the temperate style does not need the grand style, for it is used for purposes of delight rather than for persuasion.

XXIV

53. If a speaker is applauded frequently and vigorously, he should not think that for that reason he is speaking in the grand style; for the acumen revealed in the subdued style and the ornaments of the moderate style may produce the same result. For the grand style frequently prevents applauding voices with its own weight, but it may bring forth tears. Thus when I was dissuading the populace of Caesarea in Mauretania from civil war, or rather from a war worse than civil which they called "Caterva"—for not only the citizens themselves, but relatives, brothers, even parents and children, divided themselves into two parts for several successive days at a certain time of the year and solemnly fought each other with stones, and each killed whomever he could—I pleaded in the grand style in so far as I was able that they should cast forth from their hearts and customs such a ferocious and inveterate evil. But I did not think that I had done anything when I heard them applauding, but when I saw them weeping. They indicated by applause that they were being taught or pleased, but tears indicated that they were persuaded. When I saw these, I believed that the terrible custom handed down by their fathers and grandfathers and from still more remote times, which had besieged their hearts like an enemy, or rather taken them, had been overcome, even before the victory had been demonstrated. As soon as the speech was finished, I directed their hearts and lips to giving thanks to God. And behold! by the grace of Christ, nothing similar has been attempted there

for eight years or more. There are many other experiences through which we have learned what effect the grand style of a wise speaker may have on men. They do not show it through applause but rather through their groans, sometimes even through tears, and finally through a change of their way of life.

54. And many are changed through the subdued style, but in such a way that they know what they did not know before, or believe what they did not formerly believe, not in such a way that they do what they know they should do, although they have not desired to do so. To bend hardness of this kind the grand style is necessary. But when praises and vituperations are eloquently spoken, although they belong to the moderate style, they so affect some that they are not only delighted by the eloquence of praising or blaming, but also desire to live in a praiseworthy way and to avoid living in a way that should be blamed. But is it true that all who are delighted are changed as in the grand style all who are persuaded act, or in the subdued style all who are taught know, or believe to be true, what they did not know before?

XXV

55. Hence it is to be concluded that the purpose that these two styles seek to effect is especially important to those who would speak with wisdom and eloquence. That which the moderate style urges, that is, that the eloquence itself be pleasing, is not to be taken up for its own sake, but in order that things which may be usefully and virtuously spoken, if they require neither a teaching nor a moving eloquence, may have a knowing and sympathetic audience which sometimes may assent more readily or adhere more tenaciously to that which is being said because of the delight aroused by that eloquence. For it is the universal office of eloquence, in any of these three styles, to speak in a manner leading to persuasion; and the end of eloquence is to persuade of that which you are speaking. In any of these three styles an eloquent man speaks in a manner suitable to persuasion, but if he does not persuade,

he has not attained the end of eloquence. Thus in the subdued style he persuades his listener that what he says is true;
he persuades in the grand style that those things which we
know should be done are done, although they have not been
done. He persuades in the moderate style that he himself
speaks beautifully and with ornament. Of what use is this to
us? Let those seek this end who glory in their language, and
who display themselves in panegyrics and other speeches of
this kind, neither moving the listener to do anything nor
teaching him anything, but simply pleasing him. We, however, refer this end to another end, that is, so that in addition
to what we desire to bring about when we speak in the grand
style we also desire this: that good habits be loved and evil
avoided. Or, if men are seen not to be so hostile to the action
which we are urging that the grand style is necessary, or if they
are already practicing it, that they do so more assiduously we
use the moderate style. Thus we use the ornaments of the
moderate style not ostentatiously but prudently, not content
with its end that the audience be pleased, but rather using
them in such a way that they assist that good which we wish
to convey by persuasion.

XXVI

56. Thus those three ends which we described above for a
man who speaks wisely if he would also speak eloquently, that
is, that he should so speak that he is heard intelligently, willingly, and obediently, are not to be taken so that one of the
three styles is attributed to each one so that the subdued style
pertains to understanding, the moderate style to willingness,
and the grand style to obedience; rather, in such a way that the
orator always attends to all three and fulfills them all as much
as he can, even when he is using a single style. We do not
wish to tire the listener, even when we speak in the subdued
style, but we desire rather that he hear not only intelligently
but also willingly. And why do we employ divine testimonies
in what we say in order to teach, except that we may be heard

obediently, that is, that we may be believed with the aid of Him to whom it is said, "Thy testimonies are become exceedingly credible"? [1] What does he desire who explains something to learners even in the subdued style but to be believed? And who would wish to hear him unless he could retain his listener with some sweetness of discourse? Who does not know that, if he is not heard with understanding, neither is he heard willingly or obediently? Frequently the subdued style, when it solves difficult questions and demonstrates in unexpected ways, when it brings to light and sets forth most acute principles from I know not what caverns, as it were, in an unexpected way, when it shows an adversary's error and reveals that what he seemed to say uncontrovertibly is false, and especially if a certain beauty is added to it, not deliberately sought but in some way natural, and a few rhythmic closings are used, not ostentatiously but, as I say, as if necessary, arising from the things discussed themselves, then it excites such acclamations that it is hardly recognized as being subdued. It does not come forth armed or adorned but, as it were, nude, and in this way crushes the sinews and muscles of its adversary and overcomes and destroys resisting falsehood with its most powerful members. Why is it that those using this style are frequently and greatly applauded unless for the reason that truth thus demonstrated, defended, and placed in triumph is a source of delight? And in this subdued style our teacher and speaker should so conduct himself that he is heard not only intelligently but also willingly and obediently.

57. And that moderate style of eloquence when used by our eloquent churchman should neither be left unornamented nor be ornamented indecently. Nor should it seek only to please, as it does exclusively among other orators. Rather in maintaining that those things which it praises are to be desired or firmly adhered to, and that those things which it blames are to be avoided and held in contempt, it wishes also to be obediently heard. But if it is not heard with understanding it cannot be heard willingly. Indeed, even in that style which

1 Ps. 92. 5 [93. 5].

has delight as its end, it is to be sought that those who hear understand, that they are delighted, and that they obey.

58. Now when it is necessary to move and bend the listener by means of the grand style (which is necessary when he will confess that the speech is true and agreeable, but will not do what it says should be done), one must undoubtedly speak grandly. But who is moved if he does not know what is being said? Or who is held attentive that he may hear if he is not delighted? Whence also in this style, where the hard heart is to be bent to obedience through the grandness of the diction, if what is heard is not heard intelligently and willingly, it cannot be heard obediently.

XXVII

59. However, the life of the speaker has greater weight in determining whether he is obediently heard than any grandness of eloquence. For he who speaks wisely and eloquently, but lives wickedly, may benefit many students, although, as it is written, he "is unprofitable to his own soul." [1] Whence the Apostle also said, "Whether as a pretext, or in truth [let] Christ be preached." [2] For Christ is the Truth, and, moreover, the truth may be announced but not in truth, that is, evil and fallacious hearts may preach what is right and true. Thus indeed is Jesus Christ announced by those who "seek the things that are their own, not the things that are Jesus Christ's." [3] But since the good faithful do not obey any man, but obediently hear that Lord who said "All things therefore whatsoever they shall say to you, observe and do: but according to their works do ye not; for they say, and do not," [4] thus they may hear usefully those who do not act usefully. They seek their own ends but do not dare to teach their own doctrines, at least not from the high place of ecclesiastical authority which sound doctrine has constituted. On this account Our Lord, before He spoke of those I have mentioned, said by way of introduc-

[1] Ecclus. 37. 21.
[2] Phil. 1. 18.
[3] Phil. 2. 21.
[4] Matt. 23. 3.

tion, "[They] have sitten on the chair of Moses." [5] Thus that chair, not their own but that of Moses, forced those to speak well who did not also act well. They did what they would in their lives, but the chair of another did not permit them to teach their own doctrines.

60. And thus they benefit many by preaching what they do not practice; but many more would be benefited if they were to do what they say. For there are many who seek a defense of their evil lives in those of their superiors and teachers, responding in their hearts or, if it breaks forth so far, with their lips, and saying, "Why do you not do what you preach that I do?" Thus it happens that they do not obediently hear one who does not hear himself, and they condemn the word of God which is preached to them along with the preacher himself. Hence, when the Apostle, writing to Timothy, said, "Let no man despise thy youth," he added the reason why he was not to be despised and said, "but be thou an example of the faithful in word, in conduct, in charity, in faith, in chastity." [6]

XXVIII

61. A teacher with these virtues, in order that he may be obediently heard, speaks without shame not only in the subdued and moderate style but also in the grand style because he does not live contemptibly. He chooses a good life in such a way that he does not also neglect good fame, but provides "what may be good not only before God, but also before men" [1] in so far as he is able by fearing God and caring for men. In his speech itself he should prefer to please more with the things said than with the words used to speak them; nor should he think that anything may be said better than that which is said truthfully; nor should the teacher serve the words, but the words the teacher. This is what the Apostle meant by "not in wisdom of speech, lest the cross of Christ should be made void." [2] What he said to Timothy is also perti-

5 Matt. 23. 2.
6 1 Tim. 4. 12.

1 2 Cor. 8. 21.
2 1 Cor. 1. 17.

nent to this: "Contend not in words, for it is no profit but to
the subverting of the hearers." [3] Nor is this said in order that
we should say nothing for truth against adversaries opposing
truth. For where then would be what he said, among other
things, when he was showing what sort of man a bishop
should be: "that he may be able to exhort in sound doctrine,
and to convince the gainsayers"? [4] For to contend in words
is not to care how error is overcome by truth, but how your
speech is preferred to that of another. Indeed, he who does
not dispute in words whether he uses the subdued, the moderate, or the grand style, so acts with words that the truth becomes clear, that the truth is pleasing, and that the truth
moves. For charity itself, which is the end and fulfillment of
the Law, cannot be right if those things which are loved are
not true but false. Just as he whose body is beautiful while his
mind is deformed is more to be pitied than he whose body
is also deformed, in the same way those who speak false things
eloquently are more to be pitied than if they had said the
same things awkwardly. What, therefore, is it to speak not only
wisely but also eloquently except to employ sufficient words
in the subdued style, splendid words in the moderate style, and
vehement words in the grand style while the things spoken
about are true and ought to be heard? But he who cannot do
both should say wisely what he cannot say eloquently rather
than say eloquently what he says foolishly.

XXIX

However, if he cannot do this, let him so order his life that he
not only prepares a reward for himself, but also so that he
offers an example to others, and his way of living may be, as
it were, an eloquent speech.

62. There are some who can speak well but who cannot
think of anything to say. If they take something eloquently
and wisely written by others, memorize it, and offer it to the

3 2 Tim. 2. 14.   4 Titus 1. 9.

people in the person of the author, they do not do wickedly. In this way, which is truly useful, many preachers of the truth are made, but not many masters, if they all speak the words of the one true Master and are not schismatics. Nor are they to be deterred by these words in the voice of Jeremias the prophet, through whom God reproves those "who steal my words every one from his neighbor." [1] For those who steal take something from another, but the word of God is not another's to those who obey it; rather, he speaks another's word who, when he speaks well, lives evilly. For whatever good things he says seem to have been the products of his own thought, but they are actually alien to his behavior. Thus God said that they steal His words who wish to seem good, speaking those things which are God's, when at the same time they are evil, doing the things that are theirs. Nor do such people actually say the good things which they pretend to, if we consider the matter carefully. How do they say something with words which they deny with deeds? The Apostle did not say vainly of such persons "They profess that they know God, but in their works they deny him." [2] In a certain way they speak, but in another way they do not speak, since both things are true which Truth said. Speaking of such persons, "What they say," He says, "do: but according to their works, do ye not"; that is, what you hear from their lips, do; what you see in their works, do not do. "They say," He says, "and do not." [3] Thus, although they do not act, they speak. In another place, condemning such men, He said, "Hypocrites, how can you speak good things, whereas you are evil?" [4] Accordingly those things which they say when they speak good things they do not themselves say, denying in will and deed what they say. Whence it may happen that an evil and wicked man may compose a sermon in which truth is preached which is spoken by another not wicked but good. And when this is done, the wicked man hands down to another what is not his own, and the good man accepts

---

[1] Jer. 23. 30.
[2] Titus 1. 16.
[3] Matt. 23. 3.
[4] Cf. Matt. 12. 34.

what is his from another. But when the good faithful perform this work for others who are good and faithful, both speak what is their own, for God is theirs, and those things which they speak are His. They make their own those things which they themselves could not compose when they live in accordance with them.

XXX

63. Whether one is just now making ready to speak before the people or before any other group or is composing something to be spoken later before the people or to be read by those who wish to do so or are able to do so, he should pray that God may place a good speech in his mouth. For if Queen Esther prayed, when she was about to address the king concerning the temporal welfare of her people, that God would place "a well ordered speech" [1] in her mouth, how much more ought he to pray for such a reward who labors in word and teaching for the eternal salvation of men? Those also who are about to speak what is delivered to them from others should pray for those from whom they receive it, before they receive it, that they may be given what they wish to receive. And when they have received it, they should pray that they may deliver it well, and that those to whom they offer it may take it; and for the profitable result of their speech they should give thanks to Him from whom they should not doubt they have received it, so that he who glories may glory in Him in whose "hand are both we and our words." [2]

XXXI

64. This book has turned out longer than I wished, and longer than I had thought it would be. But to that reader or listener to whom it is pleasing it is not long. He who finds it long and wishes to know about it may read it in sections. He who does not wish to know about it, however, should not com-

---

1 Esther 14. 13.   2 Wisd. 7. 16.

plain about its length. I nevertheless give thanks to God that in these four books I have discussed with whatever slight ability I could muster, not the kind of man I am, for I have many defects, but the kind of man he ought to be who seeks to labor in sound doctrine, which is Christian doctrine, not only for himself, but also for others.